Player's Manual

for use with

The Business Strategy Game
A Global Industry Simulation

Seventh Edition

Arthur A. Thompson, Jr.
The University of Alabama

Gregory J. Stappenbeck
The University of Alabama

McGraw-Hill
Irwin

Boston   Burr Ridge, IL   Dubuque, IA   Madison, WI   New York   San Francisco   St. Louis
Bangkok   Bogotá   Caracas   Kuala Lumpur   Lisbon   London   Madrid   Mexico City
Milan   Montreal   New Delhi   Santiago   Seoul   Singapore   Sydney   Taipei   Toronto

McGraw-Hill Higher Education

A Division of The **McGraw-Hill** *Companies*

Player's Manual for use with
THE BUSINESS STRATEGY GAME: A GLOBAL INDUSTRY SIMULATION
Arthur A. Thompson, Jr. and Gregory J. Stappenbeck

1 2 3 4 5 6 7 8 9 0 QPD/QPD 0 9 8 7 6 5 4 3 2 1 0

ISBN 0-07-237567-1

www.mhhe.com

Contents

Contents (continued)

The Industry and the Company

Welcome to *The Business Strategy Game*! You are joining the senior management team at a $100 million company making athletic footwear. The company's product line is gaining in popularity and the global athletic footwear industry presents some interesting growth opportunities in the world's four major geographic markets—North America, Asia, Europe, and Latin America—and in the newly-emerging online sales segment. You and your co-managers have the challenge of developing and executing a strategy that will propel the company into a prominent and profitable position in the global athletic footwear industry over the next 5 to 10 years. Your company will be in head-to-head competition with a number of other companies pursuing the market potential in athletic footwear and striving for industry leadership.

In playing *The Business Strategy Game*, you and your co-managers will need to address a number of strategic and operating issues facing your company. Immediate problems include making the company's recent venture into online sales at the company's Web site a profitable success, dealing with high production costs at the company's Texas plant, and deciding whether to go forward with plans to enter the Latin American market. Longer range, the challenge will be how to build a sustainable competitive advantage, counter the strategic moves of rival companies, and build long-term value for the company's shareholders.

You and your co-managers will have full authority over the company's selling prices, product quality, customer service effort, advertising, product line breadth, retail outlet network, promotional rebate offers, and online sales at the company's Web site, thus giving you an array of competitive strategy options in each market arena in which you decide to compete. It will be entirely up to you and your co-managers to decide how to try to out-compete rival companies—whether to strive to become the industry's low-cost producer and use your low-cost advantage to undersell competitors, whether to differentiate your company's footwear lineup on the basis of quality or service or other attributes, and whether to compete worldwide or to focus on just one or two market segments. You can elect to position the company in the low end of the market, the high end, or stick close to the middle on price, quality, and service. You can put the marketing emphasis on brand-name footwear or you can stress sales to private-label retailers. You can concentrate on selling through independent footwear retailers or you can shift more emphasis to online sales and/or company-owned retail megastores. You can stick with the company's current North American and Asian production bases or you can build new plants in Europe and/or Latin America. And, you can finance the company's growth with whatever mix of cash, short-term loans, long-term bonds, or new issues of common stock that you deem appropriate. Whichever long-term direction and business strategy is chosen, you and your co-managers will be held accountable for achieving acceptable financial performance, increasing shareholder value, and making the company a respected industry leader. The success your executive team has in managing the company will be based on how well your company compares against other companies on six performance measures: sales revenues, after-tax profits, return on investment, bond rating, stock value, and strategy rating.

Each decision period in *The Business Strategy Game* represents a year. Very likely, you and your co-managers will be asked to make anywhere from 6 to 12 complete sets of decisions, meaning that you will be in charge of the company for 6 to12 years—long enough to test your strategy-making, strategy-implementing skills. Expect the action to be fast-paced and exciting as industry conditions change and as companies jockey for market position and competitive advantage.

What You Can Expect to Learn

The Business Strategy Game is a hands-on learning exercise designed to:

- Deepen your understanding of revenue-cost-profit relationships and the factors that drive profitability.

- Provide an integrative, capstone experience.

- Enhance your understanding of the strategies for competing successfully in globally competitive and e-commerce environments.

- Provide valuable decision-making practice and help you develop good business judgment.

Gaining a Deeper Understanding of Revenue-Cost-Profit Relationships. Playing *The Business Strategy Game* will boost your understanding of basic revenue-cost-profit relationships and the factors that drive profitability. The what-ifing and numerical analysis that you'll find essential in operating your company in a businesslike manner will help you gain greater command of the numbers commonly found in company financial and operating reports. You'll get valuable practice in reviewing operating statistics, identifying costs that are out-of-line, comparing the profitability of different market segments, assessing your company's financial condition, and deciding on what remedial and proactive approaches to take. Since the simulation is played on personal computers, the nitty-gritty number crunching is done in a split second. You'll be able to see the revenue-cost-profit impact of each decision entry, making it easy to explore alternative "what-if" scenarios and determine which of several different strategy options and decision combinations seems to offer the best profit potential. There's an option to construct a strategic plan and evaluate which of several longer-range strategies is more attractive. The power of having the computer instantaneously calculate the consequences of each decision will make you appreciate the importance of basing decisions on solid number-crunching analysis instead of the quicksand of "I think", "I believe", and "Maybe it will work out OK."

Consolidating Your Knowledge and Skills: An Integrative, Capstone Learning Experience. *The Business Strategy Game* incorporates much of what you have studied in your production, marketing, finance, accounting, human resources, and economics courses. The company you will be managing has plants to operate, work forces to hire and pay, inventories to control, marketing and sales campaigns to wage, prices to set, a Web site and online sales channel to manage, accounting and cost data to examine, capital expenditure and investment decisions to make, shareholders to worry about, sales volumes to forecast, tariffs and exchange rate fluctuations to consider, and ups and downs in interest rates and the stock and bond markets to take into account. The simulation involves as many as 195 decision entries each period and 85 what-if entries to forecast unit sales. Wrestling with so many decision variables will not only give you a stronger understanding of how all the different functional pieces of a business fit together but also teach you the importance of looking at decisions from a ***total-company perspective*** and unifying decisions in a variety of functional areas to create a cohesive strategic action plan. You'll see why and how decisions made in one area spill over to affect outcomes in other areas of the company. The simulation is very much a capstone learning experience that ties together the information and analytical tools covered in earlier courses.

Understanding the Functioning of Globally Competitive Markets and the Economics of E-tailing. *The Business Strategy Game* will give you much deeper insight into the ins and outs of global competition, the different strategies companies can pursue in world markets, and the challenges of competing in a global market environment. We have designed *The Business Strategy Game* to be as realistic and as faithful to the functioning of a worldwide competitive market as a computerized simulation exercise can be. The game brings into play many of the business issues and competitive conditions characteristic of today's global markets. Your company will have to contend with exchange rate fluctuations, tariff barriers, and cross-country production cost differences. You will have to decide whether to locate plants where wage rates are low or whether to avoid import tariffs by having a production base in each primary geographic market. You will have to decide whether to use much the same competitive strategy worldwide or whether to customize your strategy to specific conditions in the North American, European, Latin American, and Asian markets. Furthermore, you'll be able to experiment with the use of a "bricks-and-clicks" e-tailing strategy—the company you'll be managing has recently begun selling its products online.

Learning to Make Sound Decisions and to Exercise Good Business Judgment. *The Business Strategy Game* will give you valuable decision-making practice and help you learn to exercise good business judgment. The simulation involves as many as 195 decision entries each period and 85 what-if entries to forecast unit sales. Dealing with so many decision variables and business issues simultaneously will not only give you a stronger understanding of how all the different functional pieces of a business fit together, but also cause you to appreciate the value of making decisions from a companywide perspective. In making the strategic and operating decisions that arise in the simulation, you and your co-managers will encounter an array of fairly typical business issues and decision situations. You'll have to assess changing industry and competitive conditions, diagnose the strategies of competitors and anticipate their next moves, pursue ways to secure a competitive advantage, evaluate different courses of action, chart a strategic course for your company to take, and adjust strategic plans in response to changing conditions. There will be ample opportunities to gain proficiency in using the concepts and tools of strategic analysis. You will learn what it means to "think strategically" about a company's competitive market position and the kinds of actions it will take to improve it. As your skills in "market-watching" and "competitor-watching" get sharper, your sense of business judgment about how to strengthen a company's competitive position and financial performance will improve. You will get to test your ideas about how to run a company, and there will be prompt feedback on the caliber of your decisions.

Preparing You for the Game of Business in Real Life and Stimulating Your Competitive Spirit. In sum, playing *The Business Strategy Game* will draw together the lessons and information of prior courses, build your confidence in analyzing the revenue-cost-profit economics of a business, help you understand how the functional pieces of a business fit together, give you valuable practice in crafting profitable growth strategies, and sharpen your business judgment. You will gain needed experience and practice in assessing business risk, analyzing industry and competitive conditions, making decisions from a companywide perspective, thinking strategically about a company's situation and future prospects, developing strategies and revising them in light of changing conditions, and applying what you have learned in business school. The bottom line is that playing *The Business Strategy Game* will make you better prepared for playing the game of business in real life. We predict that in the process your competitive spirit will be stimulated and that you will have a lot of fun.

The Company You Will Manage

Your company began footwear manufacturing operations ten years ago in a converted two-story warehouse in Cincinnati using makeshift equipment. John Delgaudio, Richard Tebo, and Sam Ruggles—the three co-founders—developed a modestly innovative line of athletic footwear and then proceeded over the next ten years to transform their fledgling Ohio-based enterprise into an $100 million public company with budding opportunities in the global market for athletic-style shoes. The company has two plants—a 1 million pair per year plant outside San Antonio and a new state-of-the-art Asian plant that can turn out 3 million pairs annually. Distribution warehouses have been opened in the United States (in Memphis, Tennessee), in Europe (Brussels, Belgium), and in Asia (Singapore) to serve the world's three biggest geographic markets. The company's stock price has risen from $5.00 in Year 7, when the company went public, to $15 at the end of Year 10. The stock is traded in the over-the-counter market (NASDAQ); there are 6 million shares of the company's stock outstanding.

The company was founded 10 years ago by John Delgaudio, Richard Tebo, and Sam Ruggles to manufacture and market running and jogging shoes. John and Richard had tried various brands of shoes while members of the track team at a well-known mid-western university. Both had experienced shoe-related difficulties of one sort or another and felt that no company made shoes that provided good foot protection and that performed well under the conditions encountered in cross country running and in long-distance marathons run on hard pavement. Long discussions about what they were going to do after graduation led them to think about forming a small company of their own to develop and market a new-style shoe line with features that would be welcomed by runners and serious joggers.

John's father had been a manufacturer's representative for one of the traditional athletic equipment companies ever since John was in the second grade. When John and

Richard began to talk in earnest about starting their own athletic shoe company, John's father arranged for John and Richard to spend a day touring one of the New England shoe plants affiliated with the athletic equipment manufacturer he represented. During the tour, John and Richard met Sam Ruggles, who at age 32 had risen quickly through the ranks to become plant manager. Sam had a degree in mechanical engineering and was fascinated with machinery and the technical manufacturing aspects of the athletic footwear-making process. The three young men hit it off well together, and John and Richard immediately decided to invite Sam to join them in exploring the possibility of setting up their own company.

Two months after John and Richard graduated, plans for the new company were in high gear. Hours of brainstorming and intensive study of shoes then on the market produced three shoe designs with features no other manufacturer had. One feature involved a special air cushion sole, another involved the use of a waterproof fabric that breathed and wicked away foot perspiration, and a third involved a new type of heel support. Sam's technical know-how proved invaluable in drawing up designs and figuring out how to manufacture the shoes. Meanwhile, John located a building on the outskirts of Cincinnati that was being vacated and some used manufacturing equipment in reasonably good condition, all of which could be leased for $7,500 per month with an option to buy. The three partners contributed $50,000 in equity capital and secured a $100,000 loan from Richard Tebo's well-to-do parents.

The First Five Years. The company was formally incorporated in August, with each founder having a one-third ownership. John Delgaudio functioned in the role of president and handled the financial and administrative chores; Richard Tebo took charge of the distribution and sales functions; and Sam Ruggles assumed responsibility for product design, purchasing, and manufacturing operations. The first pair of shoes rolled off the production line in mid-October, and the first shipment to a retail dealer was personally delivered by Richard Tebo in time for the Christmas shopping season.

The first two years were a struggle—long hours were spent testing various features and types of materials, perfecting shoe designs for different activities (jogging, walking, tennis, and aerobics), working the bugs out of the makeshift equipment and plant setup, demonstrating the shoes to dealers, and convincing dealers to handle the company's shoe line. Hundreds of pairs were given away free to high school athletes to try; Tebo spent many hours listening to user reactions and monitoring how well the shoes held up under wear and tear. The company lost money in its first year and had to use nearly $92,000 of the $100,000 loan extended by Richard Tebo's parents. But the shoes coming off the assembly line were looking better, manufacturing efficiency was improving, and reaction to the company's shoes was positive. In the second year of operation, the company sold a total of 28,000 pairs and revenues topped $500,000. Most of the sales were to independent retail dealers in the southern Ohio and northern Kentucky areas. Richard Tebo's persistence in calling on these dealers frequently, explaining the features of the shoe models to them, and even assisting the store clerks in selling customers on the shoes was a big factor in giving the company a market toehold.

In the company's third year of operation, cash flows improved and the company's financial status grew less precarious. Pairs sold topped 150,000 and revenues surpassed the $3 million mark. The founders plowed all their profits back into the business, concentrating on designing more models and broadening geographic distribution. As teenagers and young adults began to wear athletic-style shoes for everyday, walking-around purposes, the company started marketing to retail shoe stores as well as sporting goods and athletic apparel stores. A line of walking shoes for men and women was introduced.

By the company's fourth year of operation, market demand for athletic footwear started to take off in the United States and Europe. The rising price of leather shoes made fabric shoes an attractive money-saving option. At the same time, dress styles were becoming more casual among adults, and more people of all ages were taking up jogging, walking, aerobics, and regular exercise. Athletic footwear became a standard item in people's personal wardrobes. A comfortable casual-wear line of shoes for men, women, and children was introduced. In Year 5, demand for the company's brand jumped to 475,000 pairs and revenues rose to $17 million. Meanwhile, to accommodate rising sales and improve production efficiency, the decision was made to relocate the company's production facilities to the outskirts of San Antonio, Texas, where a then state-of-the-art 1 million-pair plant was constructed at a cost of $20 million and financed largely with long-term debt. The co-founders saw San Antonio as an attractive plant location because of the ready availability of nonunion labor and the strong work ethic of area residents. A central distribution center was leased in Memphis, Tennessee, to handle all shipments to retail dealers in North America.

The Second Five Years. Over the last five years, the company's footwear sales have expanded fivefold to almost 2.5 million pairs; revenues for Year 10 totaled $99.3 million. To achieve this growth, the company took some aggressive steps. The company leased a warehouse in Brussels, Belgium, to handle distribution of the company's brands throughout the European Community; sales to European retailers began late in Year 6, eight months after the San Antonio plant came on line. In Year 8, the co-founders decided to expand again, this time opting to construct a 1 million-pair plant with state-of-the-art manufacturing equipment in Asia, where the majority of the world's athletic footwear was being produced. Asia had become the world's most popular place to manufacture athletic footwear in the 1990s because the region's lower wage rates, coupled with good labor productivity, greatly reduced labor costs per pair produced (as compared to footwear plants in North America and much of Europe). Also in Year 8 the company began to supply private-label athletic footwear to such North American retail chains as Sears, JC Penney, Wal-Mart, and Kmart on a competitive bid basis; the company used the Memphis warehouse to handle shipments to private-label customers.

A distribution center in Singapore was opened to handle sales to dealers in Japan, South Korea, China, Taiwan, Hong Kong, Indochina, Malaysia, Australia, New Zealand, and other countries in Southeast Asia; sales to dealers in the Asian Pacific began on a small scale in Year 8 and accelerated in Year 9. To accommodate rising demand, the Asian plant was expanded to 3 million pairs per year in Year 9.

To finance the company's rapid expansion program, the company went public in Year 7; 2 million shares were sold to outside investors at a net of $5.00 each. An additional 1 million shares were issued early in Year 9 to help finance expansion into Asia and to provide needed working capital. The co-founders own a combined 3 million shares, giving the company a total of 6 million shares of stock outstanding. The stock sale proceeds, along with a $17 million bond issue in Year 7 and another $13 million bond issue in Year 9, were used to finance construction and expansion of the Asian plant and launch the start-up of the company's Web site.

Exhibit 1-1 summarizes the company's performance for Years 6 through 10—*all figures are in thousands* except for earnings per share and dividends per share. As you can see, the company's growth has been profitable. Earnings per share have risen at a brisk clip, from $0.41 in Year 7 to $1.50 in Year 10. Return on net investment (ROI) is a respectable 14.4%, down a little from the previous year. The company is in good financial shape and has a strong BBB bond rating on its three outstanding bond issues.

Exhibit 1-1
Company Performance Summary, Years 6-10

		Year 6	Year 7	Year 8	Year 9	Year 10
Income Statement Summary:						
Sales Revenues —	Branded	$31,958	$41,662	$55,194	$68,640	$83,580
	Private-Label	4,990	9,012	9,485	14,170	17,000
	Total	36,948	50,675	64,679	82,810	100,580
Operating Costs –	Manufacturing	25,987	34,094	43,706	50,433	52,909
	Warehouse	4,034	5,079	6,318	10,407	12,589
	Marketing	2,063	2,913	3,624	6,081	12,492
	Administrative	1,556	2,169	2,328	2,500	3,900
	Total	33,641	44,256	55,976	69,420	81,890
Operating Profit (Loss)		3,307	6,419	8,703	13,390	18,690
Interest Income (Expense)		(347)	(1,774)	(1,584)	(2,702)	(5,833)
Income (Loss) Before Taxes		2,960	4,645	7,119	10,687	12,857
Income Taxes		888	1,394	2,136	3,206	3,857
Net Income (Loss)		$2,072	$3,252	$4,983	$7,481	9,000
Financial Performance Summary:						
Ending Cash Balance		$1,954	$2,874	$1,397	$311	$33
Total Assets		44,785	46,960	65,208	69,242	108,682
Net Investment in Property, Plant, and Equipment		19,500	24,650	49,000	61,000	78,000
Long-Term Debt		20,000	35,000	33,000	42,300	50,000
Total Liabilities		20,359	19,283	33,297	31,850	55,880
Total Stockholders' Equity		$24,426	$27,677	$31,911	$37,392	$52,802
Shares of Stock Outstanding		5,000	5,000	5,000	6,000	6,000
Earnings Per Share		$0.41	$0.65	$1.00	$1.25	$1.50
Dividends Per Share		$0.00	$0.00	$0.15	$0.20	$0.40
Return On Investment (ROI)		5.7%	11.3%	10.7%	15.5%	14.4%
Operating Profit Margin		8.9%	12.7%	13.5%	16.2%	18.6%
After-Tax Profit Margin		5.6%	6.4%	7.7%	9.0%	9.1%
Debt-To-Asset Ratio		0.45	0.75	0.51	0.61	0.46
Times-Interest-Earned			3.62	5.49	4.96	3.20
Bond Rating			BB	A	BBB	BBB
Year-End Stock Price			$6.38	$8.87	$12.25	$15.00

(handwritten margin notes: "→ need to grow private label for lower income brackets"; "→ does not reflect mktg."; "Double marketing")

The three co-founders have now decided to withdraw from active management of the company. While they will remain on the Board of Directors and retain their stock ownership (1 million shares each), they are turning decision-making control over to a new management team. Despite having done a creditable job of creating an innovative line of running, jogging, walking, and casual wear shoes; getting the new Asian plant operational; and launching international sales, they are uncertain what long-term strategy the company should now employ to enhance its competitive standing in the world footwear industry. Their indecision has prompted them to seek new management to run the company and decide what strategic course to pursue.

What the Board of Directors Expects

The Board of Directors has chosen you to become one of the company's new senior executives. The company's new management team will likely consist of three to five people, as determined by your instructor/game administrator. You and your co-managers will head the company over the next several years. *Each decision period in The Business Strategy Game represents a year.* Your management team will be asked to make anywhere from 6 to 10 complete sets of decisions. That means you will be in charge of the company for 6 to 10 years—long enough to test your strategy-making and strategy-implementing skills and accomplish the other learning objectives. Since the company has been in business for 10 years, *you and your co-managers will take over all decision-making responsibility beginning in Year 11*.

The co-founders and board members believe that the company is now reasonably well situated to capitalize on growth opportunities in North America, Europe, Latin America, and Asia (Australia, New Zealand, China, Japan, South Korea, and other Pacific Rim countries). And the company's new Web site provides the capability to make online sales and ship orders to consumers anywhere in the world.

The company's Board of Directors has charged you and your co-managers with **developing a strategic vision** for the company and **crafting a long-term strategy** that will produce the following results:

- Enhance the company's reputation and competitive standing in the industry.

- Grow earnings per share and produce an acceptable return on shareholder investment.

- Build shareholder value via a rising stock price and perhaps higher dividends.

- Preserve the company's financial integrity and bond rating.

The Board of Directors has given you and your co-managers broad authority to implement whatever strategic actions and operating changes you deem appropriate. You have only two constraints.

- You may not merge with another company in the industry—the Board wishes the company to remain independent.

- You are expected to comply fully with all legislative and regulatory requirements and conduct the company's business in an ethical manner.

How Your Company's Performance Will Be Judged. Your company's performance will be tracked annually and evaluated in relation to the performance of rival footwear companies. Six performance measures will be used to determine how well your company is doing:

- Growth in revenues.

- Growth in earnings per share above the present level of $1.50 per share.

- Return on investment (ROI).

- Market capitalization or market value of your company (defined as your company's current stock price multiplied by the number of shares outstanding).

- Bond rating.

- Strategy rating.

A weighted average of these six performance measures will be used to calculate an overall performance score both annually and all years played to date. The weights on these six performance measures will be announced at the beginning of the simulation.

The Industry and Competitive Environment

Your company will compete in a global market arena consisting of between 5 and 16 companies—the exact number of competing companies will be announced by your instructor/game administrator at the start of the simulation. All companies begin the simulation in precisely the same position—with equal sales, profits, plant capacity, inventories, prices, costs, product quality, marketing effort, and so on. The five-year operating history of each company in the industry is the same as that shown for your company in Exhibit 1-1. Every company in the industry is in sound financial condition and, so far, has competed successfully.

The prospects for long-term industry-wide growth in footwear sales are excellent. Athletic shoes have become the everyday footwear of choice for children and teenagers. Adults use athletic shoes for exercise and recreational activities. Many adults are wearing them for leisure and casual use, attracted by the lower prices in comparison to leather shoes, the greater comfort, and the easy-care features. The comfort aspects of athletic shoes have proved very attractive to people who spend a lot of time on their feet and to older people with foot problems. The combined effect of these factors is projected to generate strong market growth in all four major geographic markets over the next five years (Years 11 - 15):

Projected Annual Growth in Pairs Demanded, Years 11 - 15

North America	Asia	Europe	Latin America
5%-20%	15%-35%	10%-25%	15%-35%

The lower projected growth for the North American market is due to the fact that a sizable fraction of North American consumers have already purchased one or more pairs of athletic shoes, thus making sales more a function of replacement demand than first-time purchases. A more definite five-year demand forecast for the industry is being prepared and will be published in the Footwear Industry Report, a copy of which you will receive at the end of each year (beginning in Year 11).

Customers and Distribution Channels

Athletic footwear manufacturers can use any of four distribution channels to access the ultimate consumers of athletic footwear, the people who wear the shoes:

- Independent footwear retailers who carry athletic footwear—department stores, retail shoe stores, sporting goods stores, and pro shops at golf and tennis clubs.

- Company-owned and operated retail "megastores."

- Online sales at the company's Web site.

- Private-label sales to North American chain store accounts.

All manufacturers have traditionally relied heavily on independent footwear retailers as their primary distribution channel for sales of footwear carrying the company's own brand. Manufacturers built a network of retailers to handle their brand in all geographic areas where they marketed. Retailers are recruited and serviced by independent sales representatives (sometimes called manufacturer's representatives). Each company has manufacturer's reps to handle its product line exclusively in each geographic market. Their role is to call on retailers, convince them of the merits to carrying the company's brand of footwear, assist them with merchandising and in-store displays, and solicit orders. Manufacturers gain consumer awareness of their brands via in-store displays of retailers, media advertising, and word-of-mouth. Some independent retailers carry a limited number of the company models and styles; others carry close to the whole line.

Other retailers sell shoes from diff. mfrs.

The typical independent footwear retailer sells name brand shoes at a price that is double the wholesale price of manufacturers. However, mounting use of the Internet by shoppers has prompted all manufacturers to launch a Web site displaying all their models and styles and giving online shoppers the option to purchase footwear online at "introductory" prices which so far have run about $25 per pair below the standard retail price.

Megastores to sell their own footwear exclusively

While no manufacturer has yet done so, most are looking closely at the merits of opening two-level 14,000 square-foot company-operated "megastores" in shopping centers or malls where shoppers can peruse the company's entire product line and even try them out on a miniature running track and/or basketball court. These "megastores" can enhance the company's brand visibility with consumers as compared to relying on independent retailers of athletic footwear who typically carry several different brands and other types of footwear.

In the North American market only, there's a fourth distribution channel—private-label sales to large chain store accounts. Certain chains prefer to sell athletic footwear under their own label at prices roughly 20% below the suggested retail prices of manufacturers' name brands. All these chains buy their private-label footwear from manufacturers on a competitive-bid basis, subject to specifications of minimum product quality and product variety.

Customer demand for athletic footwear is diverse in terms of price, quality, and types of models. There are customers who are satisfied with no frills budget-priced shoes and there are customers who are quite willing to pay premium prices for top-of-the-line quality, multiple features, and fashionable styling. The biggest market segment consists of customers who buy athletic shoes for general wear, but there are sizable buyer segments for specialty shoes designed expressly for tennis, golf, jogging, aerobics, basketball, soccer, bowling, and so on. The diversity of buyer demand gives manufacturers room to pursue a variety of strategies—from competing across-the-board with many models and below-average prices to making a limited number of styles for buyers willing to pay premium prices for top-of-the-line quality.

Raw Materials Supplies

All of the materials used in producing athletic footwear are readily available on the open market. There are some 300 different suppliers worldwide who have the capability to furnish interior lining fabrics, waterproof fabrics and plastics for external use, rubber and plastic materials for soles, shoelaces, and high-strength thread. It is substantially cheaper for footwear manufacturers to purchase these materials from outside suppliers than it is to manufacture them internally in the relatively small volumes needed. Delivery time on all materials is a matter of no more than 48 hours, allowing manufacturers to operate on a just-in-time delivery basis.

2 types of quality
① normal wea[r]
② long wea[r]

Suppliers offer two basic grades of raw materials: normal-wear and long-wear. The use of long-wear fabrics and shoe sole materials improves shoe quality and performance, but they currently cost two-thirds more than normal-wear components. Materials for a shoe made completely of long-wear components cost $15 per pair versus a cost of $9 per pair for shoes made entirely of normal-wear components. However, *shoes can be manufactured with any percentage combination of normal-wear and long-wear materials*. All footwear-making equipment in present and future plants will accommodate a mixture of normal-wear and long-wear components.

All materials suppliers charge the going market price, and the qualities of long-wear and normal-wear materials are the same from supplier to supplier. Materials prices fluctuate according to worldwide supply-demand conditions. *Whenever worldwide shoe production falls below 90% of the footwear industry's worldwide plant capacity (not counting overtime production capability), the market prices for both normal and long-wear materials drop 1% for each 1% below the 90% capacity utilization level.* Such price reductions reflect weak demand and increased competition among materials suppliers for the available orders. Conversely, *whenever worldwide shoe production exceeds 100% of worldwide plant capacity utilization (meaning that companies, on average, are producing at overtime), the market prices for normal and long-wear materials rise 1% for each 1% that worldwide capacity utilization exceeds 100%.* Such price increases reflect strong demand for materials and greater ability on the part of suppliers to get away with charging more for essential raw materials.

> **Materials prices fluctuate according to worldwide utilization of plant capacity and the percentage use of long-wear materials.**

A second demand-supply condition causing materials prices to change is widespread substitution of long-wear materials for normal-wear materials. *Once global usage of long-wear materials passes the 25% level, the prices of long-wear materials rise 0.5% for each 1% that the percentage use of long-wear materials exceeds 25%; simultaneously, the worldwide market price of normal-wear materials will fall 0.5% for each 1% that the global usage of normal-wear materials falls below 75%.* Thus the price gap between long-wear and normal-wear materials widens as global use of long-wear materials rises above 25%.

Despite price fluctuations, materials suppliers have ample capacity to furnish whatever volume of materials that manufacturers need. No shortages have occurred in the past. Just recently, suppliers indicated they would have no difficulty in accommodating increased materials demand in the event footwear-makers build additional plant capacity to meet the growing demand for athletic-style shoes. Footwear manufacturers are thus assured of receiving all orders for normal-wear and long-wear materials no matter how much new footwear capacity is built down the road.

Manufacturing

Footwear manufacturing has evolved into a rather uncomplicated process, and the technology has matured to the point where it is well understood throughout the industry. At present, no company has proprietary know-how that translates into manufacturing advantage. The production process consists of cutting fabrics and materials to conform to size and design patterns, stitching the various pieces of the shoe top together, molding and gluing the shoe soles, binding the shoe top to the sole, and inserting the innersole and laces. Tasks are divided among production workers in such a manner that it is easy to measure individual worker output and thus create incentive compensation tied to piecework. Labor productivity is determined more by worker dexterity and effort than by machine speed; this is why *piecework incentives can induce greater output per worker*. On the other hand, there is ample room for worker error; unless workers pay careful attention to detail, the quality of workmanship in the final product suffers. *Quality control procedures at each step of the process are essential to minimizing the reject rates on pairs produced.*

Studies have shown that assembly lines are most efficient producing only one model at a time, though it is easy to produce different sizes of the same model simultaneously. To switch production over from one model to another takes several hours of set-up time and usually is done between shifts. Machine maintenance is also done between regular work shifts. There is sufficient time after allowing for maintenance and production setup for different models to accommodate overtime production up to 20% of normal production capacity. Thus a plant capable of producing 1 million pairs annually with a normal 40-hour workweek can turn out 1.2 million pairs annually with the maximum 20% use of overtime.

A plant may be operated at overtime, producing up to a maximum of 20% above normal annual production capacity.

Industry observers are predicting that companies will take a hard look at the economics of producing a bigger fraction of athletic shoes in Asian and Latin American countries where trainable supplies of low-wage labor are readily available. Wages and benefits for Asian and Latin American workers start at $2,500 annually compared to $12,000 in Europe and $18,000 or more in North America. The basic shoe-making abilities of workers in Asia, Europe, and Latin America are roughly equal since only modest labor skills are needed and training periods for workers are short. However, worker productivity levels at different plants can vary substantially due to the use of different incentive compensation plans, different production methods, and different plant automation options.

Weapons of Competitive Rivalry

Competition among footwear producers centers around 11 sales-determining variables: (1) wholesale selling price, (2) product quality, (3) use of customer rebates, (4) product line breadth, (5) advertising, (6) celebrity endorsements and brand image, (7) the number of independent retail outlets handling each company's brand, (8) the caliber of customer service provided to retail outlets, (9) the number of retail megastores that various companies have, (10) the effectiveness of the company's online sales effort at the company's Web site, and (11) customer loyalty. Each company's market share in a given geographic area (North America, Europe, Asia, Latin America) depends on how its combined use of the ten competitive weapons stacks up against the competitive effort of other companies competing in the same region. The stronger a company's overall competitive effort is relative to rival companies, the more pairs the company will sell and the larger its market share in that geographic region will be (provided, of course, that it has produced and shipped enough pairs to meet regional demand).

You'll find it essential to compete effectively against rivals—varying your prices, product quality, advertising, product line breadth, and so on—to capture a profitable market share and produce good bottom-line performance. We'll explain the role and impact of each of the 11 weapons of competitive rivalry in the next section. But what you should understand and appreciate fully here is that *The Business Strategy Game* is an interactive exercise; *the competitive atmosphere that prevails is determined entirely by the interplay among your company's decisions and those of rivals companies*—not by the computer software or by your instructor. Your company's revenues and market share will depend on how your company's competitive effort stacks up against the efforts of rivals. Since it is safe to assume that rival companies will try to outmaneuver and out-compete your company, you and your co-managers will have to watch competitors' actions closely and try to anticipate their moves when developing your company's strategy and making decisions. You will have to stay on top of changing market conditions, try to avoid being outmaneuvered and put into a competitive bind by the actions of rival companies, and make sure your footwear products are attractively priced and competitively marketed. How well your company performs will depend on how the caliber of your company's strategies and operating decisions stack up against the caliber of the strategies and decisions of rival companies.

At present, the company has no sharply defined strategy for competing. It charges an average price for its footwear, has an average quality product, provides an average level of service to retailers, has an average number of models for customers to select from, and has built an average brand name image via its advertising, retailer network, and rebate efforts. In other words, the company's shoes are not presently differentiated from those of rivals. Costs per pair are on a par with other rivals—the company is neither a low-cost producer nor a high-cost producer. The company is viewed as a "middle-of-the-road" competitor that is trying to participate across-the-board in all four segments of the world footwear market. The company has an average market share.

Closely related to the issue of how to become a more effective competitor is the issue of how to position the company's products in the global marketplace. Prior management was unsure whether the company should pursue both the branded and private-label segments and whether it made sense to strive for market leadership in North America, Europe, Asia, and Latin America simultaneously. And in trying to broaden the company's geographic market base, prior management was unsure whether the company should produce essentially the same quality shoes for all market segments or whether to make high quality shoes for one or two markets and low-quality shoes for the others. You and your co-managers will have the latitude to pursue a low-cost/low-price strategy in one market arena and a high quality/premium price/strong brand image strategy in another market arena should you choose to do so.

> Most any prudent business strategy has potential for succeeding; there is no built-in favoritism shown to one strategy over another.

You and your co-managers have the authority to pursue whatever business strategy you wish and to revise it as needed. *The Business Strategy Game* provides great leeway in crafting strategy, with *no built-in favoritism* shown to one strategy over another. Most any prudent business strategy has potential for succeeding, *provided it is not overpowered by the actions and strategies of rival companies*.

Overview of *The Business Strategy Game*

You play the simulation by entering your decisions on a series of decision screens. The computer software is programmed to instantly calculate the impact of each decision on key outcome measures and show you the results in an area on the screen below the decision entries. This "instant calc" feature of the software allows you to see the incremental effect of each decision and provides you with information to judge whether to stick with or change the decision entry. You'll discover that the software design of *The Business Strategy Game* provides you with powerful decision-making and what-ifing tools with which to explore the merits of alternative courses of action and arrive at a satisfactory plan for managing the company. When you start work on your decisions, be aggressive in experimenting with a variety of different decision entries and decision combinations. The more that you and your co-managers try out different decisions and observe the different projected outcomes that appear in the calculations section below the decision entries on the screen, the quicker you will come to understand the interconnections among the various decisions and arrive at an acceptable combination of decision entries. *No entry is final until you give your Company Data Disk containing your decisions to the instructor/game administrator.*

After each year's decisions are "processed," you will receive an assortment of reports detailing how your company fared. These reports include financial statements, cost analysis breakdowns, and reports concerning plant operations, warehouse and shipping operations, and sales and marketing activities. In addition, you will receive three reports containing information about the industry and about competitors. The company and industry reports provide information essential in assessing the results of the past year and developing next year's strategy and decisions.

Obtaining and Running the Company Program

The 7th Edition of *The Business Strategy Game* marks the beginning of the Internet era in delivering the simulation software to users. We believe use of the Internet will simplify and enhance your experience with *The Business Strategy Game*. This section of the Player's Manual leads you step-by-step through the following technical aspects of the using the simulation:

- **Obtaining the Company Program**—In the event you will **_not_** be playing the simulation on a PC in a computer lab setting where the program software is already installed, you can acquire the needed software by downloading it from the Web site.

- **Installing the Company Program**—The setup program that you download from the Web site is quick and easy to run.

- **Creating a Company Disk**—All of your company information is stored on a floppy disk for easy transfer to your instructor/game administrator. You will need a blank 3½ inch floppy disk with a label.

- **Running the Company Program**—A simple, yet powerful, point-and-click design makes running the software a breeze. You'll find the software intuitive and easy to navigate—your biggest challenge will be how to deal with crafty competitors rather than how to master use of the software.

Obtaining the Company Program

When you purchased this copy of *The Business Strategy Game* Player's Manual, you also purchased the right to download the BSG Company Program free of charge from the BSG Web site. Affixed to the inside cover of this manual is a label baring your personal Download Code. The easy-to-follow instructions on the label lead you through the download procedure.

The Download Code. When you go to download the Company Program from the BSG Web site, you will be asked to provide your Download Code. *Once the download of the program software is completed, your Download Code is automatically deactivated. Your Download Code can be used to download the BSG Company Program one time only—so be sure to download the software to the PC that you will be using regularly to play the simulation.* If later on, you should have occasion to download the BSG Company Program a second time, then you will need to see your instructor or game administrator for instructions on how to proceed.

Re-Sale of this Manual. Should you re-sell this copy of the Player's Manual to another student or to a book store, it is your responsibility to provide the buyer with your copy of the BSG software you have downloaded. A buyer of a used Player's Manual cannot download the latest BSG Company Program from our Web site because the Download Code for this manual will have been used by the original purchaser.

Installing the Company Program

Many of you will be playing *The Business Strategy Game* in a computer lab setting where the basic program software has already been installed on the PCs in the lab. If so, you can skip this section and move on to the section describing use of the Company Disk. If, however, you want to install the program software to your own PC, then you need to be aware of the following system requirements:

Operating System ... Windows 95, 98, NT, or 2000

Microsoft Excel 2000 (recommended); or Microsoft Excel 97 (some minor functional limitations may be experienced with use of this earlier version)

Microprocessor ...... 233 MHz or faster

Memory .... 64 megabytes of RAM (recommended); 48 megabytes of RAM (minimum)

Hard Disk Space .... 5 megabytes

Printer .... A Windows-compatible printer is recommended to optimize your use of the simulation exercise.

Setting Up the Company Program on Your PC. The download file from the BSG Web site is an executable setup program designed to quickly and easily install and set up the BSG Company Program on your PC. To execute the setup program you have downloaded, click **Start** and choose **Run** from your Windows Start Menu. Then type the path (where you downloaded the file to) and the file name and click **Ok**. For example, if you downloaded the file to your **C:\My Documents** folder, you would enter the following command line in the run box:

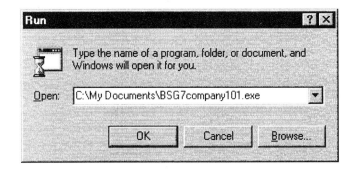

Follow the directions that appear on the screen and in a very short time *The Business Strategy Game* Company Program will be installed on your PC.

Creating a Company Disk

The Business Strategy Game consists of two separate and distinct software elements: 1) the Company Program (which is installed to the hard drive of your PC or the PCs in the computer lab), and 2) files containing specific data for your company. Your company's data consists of decision entry files (manufacturing, labor, shipping, marketing, and finance decision entries that you make each year), company report files (income statement data, balance sheet data, cash flow data, etc.), and industry data files. All of these company data files are stored in a location separate from the Company Program. Typically, your company's data will be stored on a 3½-inch floppy disk called the **Company Disk**. After you have set up the Company Program on your PC, you will be prompted with a query as to whether you want to create your Company Disk. If so, you will need to insert a blank 3½-inch floppy disk, and the Setup Program will copy all of the necessary data files onto it. If you do not have a blank floppy handy, you can come back later and create your Company Disk. (A few of you may be playing the simulation on networked computers in a computer lab setting where use of a Company Disk is unnecessary—if this is the case, your instructor/game administrator will provide you with the details and procedures. However, even here, if you want to have the capability to utilize your own PC in playing the simulation, you will need to create a Company Disk to transfer your data between PCs.)

You will need a label for your Company Disk that indicates your Industry Number (provided by your instructor/game administrator), your company letter (also provided by your instructor/game administrator). Should you inadvertently lose your Company Disk or if gets damaged *before making your first set of decisions and receiving the results back* from your instructor/game administrator, you can create a replacement disk by simply running the Setup Program again. Remember that the Setup Program creates a Company Disk updated through Year 10 and ready for Year 11 decision-making (the first year of the simulation exercise). *If you have already completed the Year 11 decision and are in Year 12 or beyond and you need to replace your Company Disk, then you must see your instructor or game administrator to obtain a replacement containing the latest company data files.*

When to Use the Company Data Folder Option. Under most circumstances, you will use a Company Disk (3½-inch floppy) to submit your decisions on and receive results back from your instructor/game administrator. However, in distance-learning situations where you are e-mailing the decisions to your instructor/game administrator and receiving results back from your instructor/game administrator, your company data can be stored on the hard drive rather than a floppy (which will allow the program to run faster), and the

Setup Program can create an appropriate data folder on your hard drive instead of a Company disk. Your annual decision entries may be delivered to your instructor/game administrator electronically via *e-mail* (see the e-mail menu item explained later in this section). *You should use the e-mail delivery function <u>only</u> if directed to do so by your instructor or game administrator.* If you are using the e-mail function *exclusively* to deliver your decisions and receive your results, then creating a data folder on your hard drive in place of a Company Disk makes sense, simply for convenience and to expedite computer processing times. *However, the e-mail decision delivery and receipt function can be used if your company data is stored on a Company Disk (3½ floppy) as well as a folder on your PC's hard drive.*

Getting Started

Launching the Program. When you installed the BSG Company Program to your PC, the Setup Program automatically created an item on your Programs Menu called *Business Strategy Game 7e.* To launch the program, click *Start, Programs, Business Strategy Game 7e*, and *BSG Company Operations.* If you cannot find the *Business Strategy Game 7e* menu item, you can launch the BSG Company Program by clicking *Start, Run*, and entering **C:\BSG7co\Main.xls** in the run box.

When you start the program, *The Business Strategy Game* title screen will appear. Insert your Company Disk in the floppy drive and click the "Continue" button. Unless otherwise directed by your instructor/game administrator because you are playing a "diskless version" of the simulation in a networked computer lab, *your Company Disk must ALWAYS be in the floppy drive when you run The Business Strategy Game.*

The First Time You Run *The Business Strategy Game***.** The first time you run the game, a "Company Identification Screen" will appear (see Exhibit 2-1). You will be asked to supply the following information:

1. Your *Industry Number* (assigned to you by your instructor/game administrator; a number from 1 to 99).

2. Your *Company Letter* (assigned to you by your instructor/game administrator; a letter from A to P).

3. Your *Company Name* (the first character of your company name must be the same as your assigned company letter; make sure your Company Name is not too long to fit in the space provided).

4. A *Ticker Symbol* under which your stock will trade on the Footwear Stock Exchange (the first character of the ticker symbol must be the same as your assigned company letter).

5. A *Company Password* (choose a password that you consider secure and yet easy to remember; BSG passwords are case-sensitive).

If you do not know your Industry Number or Company Letter (or if your instructor/game administrator has not yet assigned you an Industry Number or Company Letter), click on the "Practice" button and proceed. You can come back and enter the required ID information before completing the first decision.

If you enter wrong or incomplete Company Identification information, your decision entries will not be recognized and will be rendered invalid. So be absolutely sure that your company identification information is complete and accurate before submitting your first decision to your instructor/game administrator.

Exhibit 2-1

Company Identification Screen

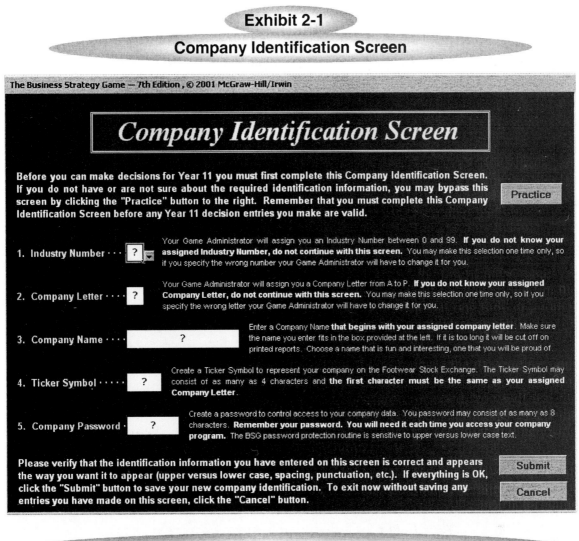

Company Identification Screen

Before you can make decisions for Year 11 you must first complete this Company Identification Screen. If you do not have or are not sure about the required identification information, you may bypass this screen by clicking the "Practice" button to the right. Remember that you must complete this Company Identification Screen before any Year 11 decision entries you make are valid.

Practice

1. Industry Number · · · [?] Your Game Administrator will assign you an Industry Number between 0 and 99. **If you do not know your assigned Industry Number, do not continue with this screen.** You may make this selection one time only, so if you specify the wrong number your Game Administrator will have to change it for you.

2. Company Letter · · · · [?] Your Game Administrator will assign you a Company Letter from A to P. **If you do not know your assigned Company Letter, do not continue with this screen.** You may make this selection one time only, so if you specify the wrong letter your Game Administrator will have to change it for you.

3. Company Name · · · · [?] Enter a Company Name **that begins with your assigned company letter.** Make sure the name you enter fits in the box provided at the left. If it is too long it will be cut off on printed reports. Choose a name that is fun and interesting, one that you will be proud of.

4. Ticker Symbol · · · · · [?] Create a Ticker Symbol to represent your company on the Footwear Stock Exchange. The Ticker Symbol may consist of as many as 4 characters and **the first character must be the same as your assigned Company Letter.**

5. Company Password · [?] Create a password to control access to your company data. You password may consist of as many as 8 characters. **Remember your password. You will need it each time you access your company program.** The BSG password protection routine is sensitive to upper versus lower case text.

Please verify that the identification information you have entered on this screen is correct and appears the way you want it to appear (upper versus lower case, spacing, punctuation, etc.). If everything is OK, click the "Submit" button to save your new company identification. To exit now without saving any entries you have made on this screen, click the "Cancel" button.

Submit

Cancel

Exploring the Menu Bar

The Business Strategy Game Menu consists of a bar across the top of the screen. As shown in Exhibit 2-2, the Menu Bar Guide Screen explains each of the items found in the Menu Bar. More than likely, you will use all of these menu items at one time or another during the course of the simulation exercise. Spend some time familiarizing yourself with the Menu Bar.

You will use the 10 decision buttons on the Menu Bar to forecast the demand for your company's products and to access the decision entries for various aspects of your company's operations. After the decisions for each year are processed, you will use the four buttons in the reports portion of the screen to view or obtain printouts of all the results for that period. You'll find the information in these reports essential in diagnosing what happened and in making decisions for the upcoming year.

Three of the four reports are contain only sample data for Year 10 (because all companies had the same prices and competitive effort and the same operating results for Year 10), and will be updated after Year 11 is processed by your instructor/game administrator. Copies of these reports going into Year 11 add nothing about competitors or industry conditions beyond what is described in the next sections of this manual. The fourth menu item in the Reports portion of the Menu Bar allows you to view or print copies of the company reports for Year 10. You may find it convenient to print a copy to refer to in making Year 11 decisions; we'll talk about the significance of the information in these reports in the upcoming sections of this manual.

Exhibit 2-2
Menu Bar Guide Screen

Decisions: ... Reports: FIR ... Analysis: ... Utility: ...

Menu Bar Guide Click on the desired icon or matching icon button at the top of the screen.

DECISIONS

DEMAND FORECAST — generate a demand forecast by region for Year 11

BUY SELL — PLANT PURCHASE/SALE/CLOSING — buy, sell, or liquidate plant capacity in Year 11

PRODUCTION & LABOR DECISIONS — set Y11 production specs and manage HR

SHIPPING DECISIONS — transfer branded pairs from plants to regional warehouses in Y11

PL MKT — PRIVATE-LABEL MARKETING DECISIONS — bid for Private-Label market share in Year 11

INTERNET MARKETING DECISIONS — direct marketing of branded pairs via internet in Y11

(B) BRANDED MARKETING DECISIONS — enter branded marketing efforts by region in Year 11

BIDS FOR CELEBRITY ENDORSEMENTS — vie for the services of international celebrities

FINANCING DECISIONS — finance Year 11 operations and manage the balance sheet

PLANT AUTOMATION & CONSTRUCTION — improve plants or build capacity for Y12

REPORTS

FIR FOOTWEAR INDUSTRY REPORT — will be updated after Year 11 results are known.

BENCHMARKING REPORT — will be updated after Year 11 results are known.

COMPETITOR ANALYSIS — will be updated after Year 11 results are known.

COMPANY REPORTS — income statement, balance sheet, cash flow report, etc.

ANALYSIS

BUILD ? — CAPACITY CONSTRUCTION ANALYSIS — assess plant construction / expansion options

STRAT PLAN — STRATEGIC PLAN — evaluate operating and strategic scenarios for Year 11–Year 13

CHART AND GRAPH — create pie charts, bar charts, line graphs, and strategic group maps

UTILITY

ID — COMPANY IDENTIFICATION — change company name, ticker symbol, and/or password

make a Company Disk (3½ floppy)

e-mail decisions to game administrator

EXIT — EXIT BSG PROGRAM — all decision entries are saved automatically

The Business Strategy Game — 7th Edition , © 2001 McGraw-Hill/Irwin   ↑ ↓   If necessary, click arrows to adjust screen to best fit.

The E-Mail Option

This option uses your existing locally installed e-mail program to send the decisions you make for a given year to your instructor/game administrator. ***Normally, you will use a Company Disk (3½ floppy) to submit decisions for a year***, but your instructor/game

administrator may direct you to use the e-mail option instead. Because Excel is a Microsoft product, ***the e-mail option works best with Microsoft Outlook or Outlook Express*** (which can be downloaded free from the Microsoft Web site). It can work with other locally installed e-mail programs as well, but ***it will not work with internet-based e-mail programs (like Hotmail) that use a browser as the e-mail interface***. In order to successfully e-mail decisions to your instructor/game administrator, the following conditions must be met:

1. Your PC must be connected to the Internet.

2. Your PCs default e-mail program must be loaded and running in the background.

3. The PCs default e-mail program must be a locally installed program, not an internet-based e-mail system.

When you invoke the e-mail option, the program will create an e-mail message and attach to it a data file containing your decisions. If for any reason the program cannot the e-mail to your instructor/ game administrator, you will receive a message telling you how to send the e-mail and the file attachment manually. You will just have to go through a few extra steps to achieve the same end.

The Remaining Sections of this Manual

Section 3 of the Player's Manual presents forecasts of market demand for athletic footwear in Years 11 and 12, describes the factors that determine each company's sales volume and market share, and discusses how to forecast the demand for your company's footwear.

In Sections 4, 5, 6, and 7 of this manual, we review the decision screens, discuss the decision entries, and explain various relationships, procedures, and "rules" you need to be aware of.

In Section 8 of the manual, we'll give you some additional information about how your company's performance will be scored, tell you about the various industry and company reports shown on the Menu Bar, and explain the strategic plan option. Section 9 discusses the procedures for making a decision and utilizing the various reports you are provided after each year's decisions are processed.

Before trying to use the software, you should read the entire Player's Manual, highlighting the key facts and explanations of relationships and interactions for easy future reference.

Competition and Demand Forecasts

Before you dig into the details of your company's operations and what decisions need to made for the year ahead, you first need to understand the big picture of the marketplace—the industry and competitive environment in which you are going to be competing. In this section we will describe what market conditions are like as you take over the company and start to think about your strategy and decisions for Year 11. We will look specifically at footwear sales projections for the next two years, explain each of the factors that determine your company's sales volume and market share, and describe the demand forecasting model that you can use to project unit sales in each market segment where you elect to compete.

Demand Projections for Years 11 and 12

Worldwide footwear demand is reliably forecasted to grow 16% in Year 11 and 22% in Year 12, with per company demand *averaging* 3,225,000 pairs in Year 11 and 3,950,000 pairs in Year 12. The forecasts for the five market segments are

	Private-Label Demand (in pairs)	Branded Demand (in pairs)				Worldwide Demand (in pairs)
		North America	Asia	Europe	Latin America	
Year 11	650,000	1,500,000	450,000	625,000	—	3,225,000
Year 12	700,000	1,650,000	575,000	725,000	300,000	3,950,000

To determine the overall size of the market your company will be competing for in Years 11 and 12, multiply the forecasted quantities per company by the number of companies in your industry.

Total market demand is equal to the per company projections in the previous table multiplied by the number of companies in your industry. Thus, if there are 10 companies in your industry, global market demand will be 32,225,000 million pairs in Year 11 and 39,500,000 in Year 12.

It is quite unlikely, however, that your company's actual sales in Years 11 and 12 will turn out to be exactly equal to the company averages. *How many pairs your company will actually sell in a given year always depends on how your company's overall competitive effort stacks up against the competitive efforts of rival companies.* Any company can sell substantially *more* than the per-company average by out-competing rival companies. Companies with attractively priced, aggressively marketed products will outsell companies having comparatively over-priced and/or under-marketed products. You will use the Demand Forecast screen (the first button in the Decisions portion of the Menu Bar—see Exhibit 2-2) to help you determine how many pairs you company will likely be able to sell, given (1) your company's competitive effort (selling prices, product quality, brand image, advertising, and so on) and (2) your estimates of the competitive effort exerted by rival companies.

While the industry sales forecasts for Years 11 and 12 (and the updated five-year forecasts you will receive in each issue of The Footwear Industry Report) should be considered very reliable information, actual industry-wide sales in any market segment can deviate from forecasted levels for either of two reasons: (1) unforeseen changes in economic conditions and consumer spending levels and (2) unusually strong or weak competitive efforts on the part of rival companies to capture the available sales volume.

The Role of the S&P 500 Index. Past experience shows that sales of athletic footwear vary up or down from the market forecast according to changes in the worldwide level of economic activity, consumer confidence, and employment levels. An important new study shows that the sizes of the deviations from forecasted demand correlate very closely with changes in the S&P 500 Index—a much-watched measure of the prices of the common stocks of 500 companies selected by Standard & Poor's.[1] When the S&P 500 has risen above the prior year's value, actual footwear demand industry-wide has consistently been *above* the forecasted amount. When the S&P 500 has dropped, footwear demand has consistently been *below* the projected volume. The bigger the up or down move in the S&P 500, the bigger the deviations from forecast have been—although the forecast has never been off by more than 10%.

The maximum effect that changes in the S&P 500 Index can have on next year's worldwide footwear demand is ±10%.

During the upcoming years, you should expect ups and downs in the S&P 500 Index to signal that actual industry sales of footwear will deviate above or below the forecast. The size of the deviation from the forecasted amount depends on how much the S&P 500 Index moves above or below the value announced by the instructor/game administrator for the previous year. If the upcoming year's S&P 500 value exceeds the prior-year value, actual market demand will be larger than forecasted market demand. The bigger the gap between the current year's and the previous year's S&P 500 value, the more the actual number of pairs demanded will exceed the forecasted volume (subject to the 10% limit). Conversely, actual market demand will fall below the forecasted demand when the current year's S&P 500 value

---

[1] *The daily changes in the S&P 500 Index can be found on the first page of the third section of* The Wall Street Journal; *it is also reported in the business section of many newspapers.*

falls below the previous year's value. Just how big a change in the S&P 500 it takes to induce each 1% deviation from the forecasted footwear volume is still unclear, but astute company managers should be able to arrive at good estimates within a short time.

The S&P 500 Index will have no impact on the Year 11 forecast, however. The S&P 500 Index value for Year 11 is the starting value; *the first impact of changes in the S&P 500 on forecasted sales potential comes in Year 12.*

The Role of Competitive Aggressiveness. Actual industry sales of athletic shoes are also a function of how aggressively all companies as a group try to capture the projected sales volumes. A *significant* drop in footwear prices can stimulate buying and cause actual sales to rise above the forecasted amounts. Likewise, if companies as a group *significantly* boost product quality or improve customer service, then sales for the year can exceed the projected amounts. *Unusually aggressive price-cutting and marketing efforts industry-wide can boost actual market volume by as much as 4% over the projected amount.*

Unusually aggressive (or weak) pricing and marketing efforts industry-wide will increase (or decrease) actual sales volumes above (or below) projected amounts.

On the other hand, *if average prices for footwear rise sharply or footwear quality drops or marketing efforts are cut to minimal levels, then buyers may not be attracted to purchase as many pairs as forecasted.* The weaker the industry's overall competitive effort, the greater the amount by which actual sales can fall below forecasted volumes. *All sales volume forecasts are based on the assumption that companies will exert competitive efforts comparable to Year 10 levels.*

The Factors that Determine Market Share

Competition among footwear producers centers around 11 sales-determining variables: (1) wholesale selling price, (2) product quality, (3) use of customer rebates, (4) product line breadth, (5) advertising, (6) celebrity endorsements and brand image, (7) the number of independent retail outlets handling each company's brand, (8) the caliber of customer service provided to retail outlets, (9) the number of retail megastores that various companies have, (10) the effectiveness of the company's online sales effort at the company's Web site, and (11) customer loyalty. Moreover, there is a customer loyalty factor that helps each company retain the business of footwear shoppers once they elect to purchase a particular brand. Each company's market share in a given geographic area (North America, Asia, Europe, Latin America) depends on how its combined use of the 11 competitive weapons stacks up against the competitive effort of other companies competing in the same region. The stronger a company's overall competitive effort is relative to rival companies, the more pairs the company will sell and the larger its market share in that geographic region will be (provided, of course, that it has produced enough pairs to meet demand). It is essential that you understand the role and impact of each of the 11 weapons of competitive rivalry.

Wholesale Selling Price. This is the most important of the 11 sales-determining factors. The higher your company's wholesale price to independent retailers, the higher the prices that retailers charge consumers. Consumers are quite knowledgeable about the retail prices of different brands, and many do comparison shopping on price before settling upon a brand to purchase. If your company's wholesale price in a geographic area is above the industry average in that area, some shoppers who otherwise are attracted to your brand will switch to lower-priced brands. The more your company's wholesale selling price is above the geographic average of all competitors, the lower your company's market share will tend to be. However, a higher-than-average selling price can be partially or wholly offset by a combination of higher product quality, better service to independent retailers, extra advertising, bigger customer rebates, the use of celebrity endorsements, the addition of more models to your company's product line, a more aggressive online sales effort, and a larger network of retail outlets and retail megastores. But the further your company's prices are above the industry average, the harder it is to overcome buyer resistance to a higher price and avoid a loss in market share.

Wholesale selling price is the most important competitive factor in the branded footwear markets.

Conversely, charging a wholesale price to retailers that is below the geographic market average of all competitors enhances the attractiveness of your company's brand, especially in the eyes of price-conscious shoppers, and can lead to market share gains at competitors' expense. The deeper the price cuts, the greater the potential sales gains unless the effects of a lower price are negated by sub-par quality, comparatively few models/styles for buyers to choose among, insufficient advertising, the absence of celebrity endorsements, and a retail network of retail outlets. *Low price alone is generally not sufficient for capturing a big market share*. Moreover, higher-priced rivals can offer customer rebates to dampen the market share losses to lower-priced rivals offering no rebates or lesser rebates.

In the private-label segment of the North American market, chain stores specify minimum quality standards and model variety for footwear-makers to meet and then buy strictly on the basis of which manufacturers bid the lowest prices.

Product Quality. The quality of shoes produced at each plant is a function of four factors: (1) the percentage of long-wear materials used, (2) current-year expenditures for quality control per pair produced, (3) cumulative expenditures for quality control per pair produced (to reflect learning and experience curve effects), and (4) the amount spent per model for new features and styling. *Efforts to boost quality by incorporating a progressively greater percentage of long-wear materials or by spending progressively greater amounts on quality control or new features and styling are subject to diminishing marginal benefits*. An independent association, the International Footwear Federation, obtains the needed data annually from all footwear plants, tests all models and brands on the market, and rates the quality of shoes produced at each plant of each company. The ratings of product quality at each plant range from a low of 0 to a high of 250; a rating of 50 or below denotes "minimal quality" and a rating of 90 to 120 is considered "satisfactory." The federation's formula for calculating product quality at each plant is complex because of diminishing marginal benefits associated with greater expenditures and effort on each quality determinant, but the approximate composition of the rating points is shown in Exhibit 3-1.

The four factors that determine product quality are:

1. **Long-wear materials percentage**
2. **Quality control expenditures per pair produced (in the current year)**
3. **Cumulative quality control expenditures per pair produced**
4. **Styling/features budget per model**

The sum of the points a plant gets on all four factors equals the plant's quality rating, subject to the 250-point limit. *The federation then takes the ratings of shoe quality at each plant and, based on where each plant's output is shipped and on the quality of pairs in unsold inventory, calculates quality ratings for each company in each market where its shoes are available for sale. Companies thus have five quality ratings—one for private-label shoes offered for sale in North America and one each for branded shoes offered for sale in North America, Europe, Asia, and Latin America.* A company's quality rating in each market segment is a *weighted average* of the product quality at the plants from which the pairs were shipped, adjusted up or down by the number and quality of any unsold pairs in inventory. For example, if a company had no unsold inventory in its European warehouse and it then shipped in 500,000 pairs from a plant with a production quality rating of 75 and 500,000 pairs from a plant with a production quality rating of 125, the company's weighted average quality rating for the 1 million pairs available for sale in Europe would equal 100. *The federation's quality rating formula also reduces the quality rating on all unsold private-label pairs by 5 points and the quality ratings on all unsold branded pairs by 10 points carried over in inventory to the following year* since they represent last year's models and styles.

The Federation's ratings of each company's shoe quality in each market segment are published annually in the Footwear Industry Report and are posted on its Web site. The qualities of various brands are often the subject of newspaper and magazine articles. Market research confirms that many consumers are well informed about the quality ratings and consider them in deciding which brand to buy. For example, if two competing brands were equally priced, most consumers would be inclined to buy the brand with the highest quality. *Other competitive factors being equal (price, retail outlets, product line breadth, advertising, and so on), companies with higher quality shoes will outsell companies with lower quality shoes*.

Product Line Breadth. Companies can elect to have a product line consisting of 50, 100, 150, 200, or 250 models or styles. To be regarded as a full-line producer, a company needs to have 250 models in its product line. A company with 50 models is looked upon as a specialty-line manufacturer. The competitive value of a broader product line is that the company can participate in more end-use segments (jogging, walking, aerobics, basketball, golf, tennis, and so on) and give customers a wider selection of shoe types and styles to choose from. In effect, the more models/styles a company has in its product line, the more consumers with reasons to consider buying one or more pairs of the company's footwear. *If all other competitive factors are equal (price, quality, service, advertising, brand image, and so on), companies with more models and styles in their product lines will outsell companies offering fewer models.*

Each plant is capable of producing 50, 100, 150, 200, or 250 models. The number of models a company has available in a given geographic region distribution center is a function of the number of models/styles produced at the plants from which the shoes were shipped. For example, if a company has 500,000 pairs of shoes available for sale in its Asian distribution center in Singapore and half of the pairs came from a plant producing 100 models and half came from a plant producing 200 models, then the weighted average number of models/styles that Asian consumers have to choose from is 150.

Customer Rebates. As an added sales inducement, manufacturers have the option of offering shoe buyers a rebate on each pair purchased from retailers. Some manufacturers offer promotional rebates and some don't. Rebates, if offered, can range from as low as $1 per pair to as much as $10 per pair. Manufacturers who give rebates provide retailers with rebate coupons to give buyers at the time of purchase. To obtain the rebate a customer must fill out the coupon and mail it to the manufacturer's distribution warehouse, along with the receipt of purchase. The customer service staff at the warehouse handles verification, check processing, and mailing the rebate. Some buyers lose the coupon or the sales receipt and other buyers, for various reasons, fail to take advantage of the rebate offering. Studies show that 15% of purchasers mail in the $1 rebate coupons; 20% mail in the $2 coupon; 25% redeem the $3 coupon; and so on up to

60% for the $10 coupon. *Other things being equal (price, quality, brand image, and so on), companies offering big rebates will outsell companies offering small rebates (or no rebates).*

Current-Year Advertising. Media advertising is used to inform the public of newly introduced models and styling and to tout the company's brand. Even though retail dealers act as an important information source for customers and actively push the brands they carry, advertising strengthens brand awareness, helps pull shoe buyers into retail stores carrying that brand, and informs people about the latest styles and models. The competitive impact of advertising depends on the size of your company's current-year advertising budget. A company's market aggressiveness in promoting its lineup of models and styles in a given geographic area is judged stronger when its annual advertising expenditures *exceed* the area average and is judged weaker the further its ad budget is *below* what rival companies are spending on average. *Other competitive factors being equal, companies with above-average current-year advertising expenditures outsell companies with below-average current advertising expenditures.*

Celebrity Endorsements and Brand Image. As in other industries, footwear companies can contract with celebrity sports figures to endorse their footwear brand and appear in company ads. Celebrity endorsements, along with the impressions and perceptions people gain from watching a company's media ads over time, combine to define how strong a brand image a company enjoys in the minds of athletic footwear buyers. Studies confirm that *a company's brand image has a significant effect on buyer purchases*.

Each year the International Footwear Federation conducts studies to determine each company's brand image and calculates each company's *image rating* in North America, Europe, Latin America, and Asia. The federation's brand image rating is based on (1) the *cumulative* amount of advertising a company has done in a given geographic area over time and (2) the combined influence of a company's celebrity endorsers. Company image ratings can range from a low of 0 to a high of 250 points, with *cumulative advertising and celebrity endorsements each representing a maximum of 125 points in the federation's image rating formula.* The influence of the company's celebrity endorsers is, of course, greatly enhanced by higher levels of current year advertising—it would make little sense to sign celebrities and then not feature them in company advertising. *The company with the largest cumulative advertising in a geographic region and the most influential celebrity lineup enjoys the strongest brand image in that region.*

The image rating is a function of:
1. **Cumulative advertising expenditures** (up to 125 points)
2. **Celebrity endorsements** (up to 125 points)

The Number of Retail Outlets. Independent retail outlets are currently the most important distribution channel. The more independent retail outlets a company has carrying its brand of shoes, the more market exposure a manufacturer has and the easier it is for consumers to find a nearby store from which to purchase the brand. While having more retail outlets is generally better than having fewer outlets, a company can still generate substantial sales in a geographic area with as few as 100 retail outlets, provided the company's shoe line is otherwise amply attractive to consumers and provided it has an attractive Web site offering for online sales and perhaps also utilizes retail megastores to supplement its network of independent shoe retailers.

Independent retailers, however, do not normally stock only one line of athletic footwear; most outlets carry three to five brands to provide customers with greater selection. It is very easy for a company to recruit more retailers to handle its brands because of the growing popularity of athletic footwear. At present, it costs $100 annually to support each retail outlet in a company's retail dealer network. This charge represents the costs of making sales calls, providing retailers with in-store promotional materials, printing catalogs showing models and prices, furnishing store clerks with sales information, and maintaining current credit ratings for each retailer. Currently, your company has 5000 North American retail outlets, 500 Asian outlets, and 1000 European outlets. *If all other competitive factors are equal, companies with larger numbers of retail outlets in a given geographic area will outsell companies with smaller retail networks.*

Retailer Support and Online Service. As part of their commitment to providing adequate service to independent retail dealers, it has been customary for all footwear manufacturers to employ a staff of customer service representatives who are available online or via telephone and fax to handle inquiries, take orders, and resolve any problems dealers are having. Footwear retailers are inclined to push the brands of those footwear manufacturers that provide them with the best customer service. Retail dealers and their store personnel want to deal with a footwear supplier that provides timely, attentive answers to questions and tries hard to resolve their problems. In an effort to help inform independent footwear retailers about the caliber of customer service provided by the various footwear manufacturers, the International Footwear Federation calculates and reports *service ratings* for each manufacturer in each geographic market. The federation's customer service ratings are a function of (1) whether a manufacturer has stocked out of certain sizes and models *in the previous year* and been unable to fill buyer orders, (2) actual delivery time achieved in the previous year on footwear orders, (3) whether a company's distribution centers devote sufficient resources to dealer support and service to provide short response times on inquiries and properly oversee the order fulfillment process, and (4) the desired delivery time targeted for the current year.

> **The four factors that determine the service rating are:**
> 1. Stockouts in the previous year
> 2. The delivery time <u>achieved</u> in the previous year
> 3. The resources devoted to handling customer inquiries and resolving customer problems in the current year
> 4. The <u>desired</u> delivery time in the upcoming year

As with the quality rating, the Federation's service rating ranges from a low of 0 to a high of 250. The federation's point system for calculating service ratings is shown in Exhibit 3-1. Each company's customer service ratings for North America, Europe, Asia, and Latin America are published annually in the Footwear Industry Report. Athletic footwear retailers and online buyers consult the federation's service ratings help them decide of which company to patronize. Independent footwear retailers, most of whom stock multiple brands of athletic footwear, are prone to put most of their in-store sales and merchandising emphasis on the brands of companies with good service ratings. The big majority of retailers do not want to spend time hassling with manufacturers about assorted service-related issues.

While retailers can easily live with a 4-week delivery time on footwear orders, manufacturers can boost their service rating by cutting the delivery times on the orders of footwear retailers to 3 weeks, 2 weeks, or 1 week. The federation considers an expenditure of $500 per independent retailer for dealer support and online services to be "standard"; companies can boost their service ratings with resource expenditures of more than $500 per dealer or can elect to economize on service costs by allocating less than $500 per dealer to their customer service effort. Stockouts above 100,000 pairs reduce the service rating; the bigger the stockout percentage, the bigger the service rating penalty. *The Federation's formula regarding stockouts calls for the maximum point penalty anytime a company's stockouts exceed 100% of branded sales* (provided the stockout is greater than 100,000 pairs). The Federation believes a severe service rating penalty is justified for 100%-plus stockouts because stockouts of such magnitude mean that a company was unable to fill over half of its orders from would-be buyers—an unacceptable condition from a customer perspective.

Exhibit 3-1

How the Three Ratings Are Calculated

Rating	Factors in the Rating	Point System and Weighting
Quality Rating (ranges from 0 to 250 points)	1. Percentage usage of long-wear materials at each plant	Ratings points for usage of long-wear materials: 0 to 90 points.
	2. Expenditures for styling and features per model per plant	Ratings points for styling and features expenditures: 0 to 90 points
	3. Current-year spending for quality control per pair produced by plant	Ratings points for current-year spending for quality control: 0 to 33 points
	4. The company's overall average expenditure for quality control per pair produced at all plants for all years (this measures the extent of the company's long-term quality control effort and reflects the potential to transfer quality know-how and effort across plants)	Ratings points for overall average quality control expenditures: 0 to 47 points
		Special Note: The federation's quality rating formula calls for reducing the quality rating on all unsold pairs carried over in inventory to the following year, since they represent last year's models and styles. Unsold private-label pairs receive a 5 point penalty and unsold branded pairs receive a 10 point penalty. Quality ratings are calculated for each plant to track quality produced, and also for each region of the world to track where the footwear of various qualities is shipped and marketed.
Image Rating (ranges from 0 to 250 points)	1. Cumulative expenditures on advertising by geographic region (all years combined)	Cumulative advertising and celebrity endorsements each represent a maximum of 125 points in the federation's image rating formula. Higher current-year advertising boosts the market impact of celebrity endorsers.
	2. Combined global influence of the company's celebrity endorsers	Image ratings are calculated for each geographic region of the world market to account for different advertising expenditures in different regions.
Service Rating (ranges from 0 to 250 points)	1. Stockouts in the previous year	Rating points: 50 points for stockouts of less than 100,000 pairs; anywhere from 50 to –128 points, depending on the size of the stockout as a percent of the company's branded sales in the region. The maximum point penalty applies anytime a company's stockouts exceed 100% of branded sales and 100,000 pairs.
	2. Delivery time to independent footwear retailers *achieved in the previous year* (4 weeks, 3 weeks, 2 weeks, or 1 week)	Rating points for delivery time achieved: 4 weeks: 0 points 3 weeks: 24 points 2 weeks: 52 points 1 week: 80 points
	3. Expenditures for dealer support and online services, using a benchmark of $500 per retail dealer as "standard"	Rating points: –33 points to 80 points
	4. Desired delivery time to independent footwear retailers *targeted for the upcoming year* (4 weeks, 3 weeks, 2 weeks, or 1 week)	Rating points for desired delivery time: 4 weeks: 0 points 3 weeks: 12 points 2 weeks: 26 points 1 week: 40 points
		Service ratings are calculated for each geographic region to account for different resource expenditures for dealer support and online services in different regions.

In Year 10, your company's service rating was 100 in North America, Asia, and Europe, determined as follows: 50 points for not having stocked out in Year 9, 24 points for achieving 3-week delivery in Year 9, 14 points for having a "standard" $500 per dealer expenditure, and 12 points for a delivery time target of 3 weeks in Year 10. A service rating of 50 denotes "minimal service" and a rating of 100 is considered "satisfactory." *Other competitive factors being equal (price, quality, and so on), companies with higher service ratings will outsell companies with lower service ratings*.

Company-Owned Retail Megastores. At present, no company has chosen to integrate forward and open its own retail outlets for branded footwear. But recent marketing research indicates that opening a chain of two-level 14,000 square-foot company-operated stores in high-traffic, upscale shopping centers and shopping malls could materially enhance the company's brand name visibility. Such high-profile stores would give a company the means of showcasing its entire lineup of models and styles (most independent footwear retailers stock only selected models and styles of any one brand) and sell branded footwear at retail prices directly to consumers rather than at wholesale to independent retail dealers. The research indicates that for company-owned stores to generate the highest customer traffic and have the greatest sales- and revenue-increasing impact, company-owned stores should be equipped with a miniature running track and a half-court basketball area where athletically-minded teenagers and young adults can put on a pair of shoes they are considering and try them out on the track or the basketball court. Moreover, store personnel need to have personalities that foster a festive, energetic in-store shopping environment and be trained to deliver attentive personal service. There's every indication that such stores generate good shopper traffic and have a strongly positive effect on unit sales volume and overall company revenues once the company opens a sufficient number of stores to achieve a critical mass. *Other competitive factors being equal (price, quality, and so on), the latest marketing research indicates that companies with more retail megastores will outsell companies with fewer such stores and will be able to charge somewhat higher overall prices.*

However, company owned and operated retail megastores pose some distribution channel conflict. Because independent retailers see such stores as cannibalizing their own sales of the company's shoes, should footwear manufacturers integrate forward into brick-and-mortar retailing they can expect growing antagonism from independent retailers—many of whom are already distressed about the company's Web site entry into online retailing. As a general rule, the more retail megastores a company opens in a particular geographic region (North America, Europe, Asia, and Latin America), the more that independent retailers will push other brands and styles of footwear and the weaker will be the sales-increasing effect of the company's independent retailer network.

The Attractiveness of the Company's Web Site and Online Sales Effort. All companies in the industry are currently offering their entire line of models and styles for sale at their Web sites. Online shoppers can go to the Web site, browse through color photos of the entire product line, read descriptions of each model and style, and place orders online. The company utilizes state-of-the art shopping cart software, has online credit card authorization, and uses the latest and best Web site security systems. Orders are forwarded to the nearest geographic distribution center where the order is picked, packed, and shipped usually within 24 hours.

At present, online sales have both pluses and minuses. The Web site allows the company to reach shoppers anywhere in the world, especially those not within easy shopping distance of a retailer stocking the company's brand. And, the company realizes more revenue per pair from selling its footwear above the price that it gets selling at wholesale to retail dealers. But independent retailers see the Web site as an attempt by the company to encroach on their business, and there's no question that some shoppers will switch their purchases from independent dealers (or retail megastores) to online purchases.

A company's online sales volume is a function of three global factors and three region-specific factors. The three global determinants of the unit volume sold online are (1) the number of different models and styles offered at the Web site, (2) the company's average retail sales price for these models and styles, and (3) speed of delivery (the four options are next-day air, 3-day air/ground, 1-week standard, and 2-week economy shipping). The three region-specific factors are product quality, image rating, and advertising in the buyer's region of the world market. Shipments to online buyers are always made from the distribution warehouse serving the buyer's geographic region. Since the average quality of footwear in each regional warehouse can vary from region to region, as can the company's image rating and advertising, it is logical that these three region-specific factors come into play in determining online sales in each part of the world market for branded footwear. ***The more favorably that your company's product quality, image rating, and advertising in a given region compare with those of rival footwear companies and the more favorably that your company's average online retail sales price, models offered, and delivery times compare with those of other online competitors, the bigger your online sales volume and online market share will be.***

In Year 10 worldwide online sales of branded footwear accounted for 10 percent of the total branded sales in North America, Europe, and Asia. Studies indicate that ***online sales of branded footwear (all companies combined) may rise to as much as 11% of total branded sales in each geographic region in Year 11 and to as much as 12% of total branded sales in Year 12.*** The online sales percentage is always the same for all four geographic regions of the world (for reasons of simplicity). At this juncture, it is uncertain what the global online percentage will be in Year 13 and beyond, but you will be provided with a 5-year forecast at the end of Year 11. However, studies indicate that ***online sales are unlikely to ever exceed 20% of total branded pairs sold in any one geographic region***. This is chiefly because most buyers want to see the shoes in person and try them on to check for both comfort and looks before they buy them.

Customer Loyalty. Once footwear shoppers begin purchasing a particular company's brand of athletic footwear, they are inclined to give that same brand fairly strong consideration in making their next purchases. While it is by no means certain that buyers will return to the same brand, there is indeed ***a modest brand loyalty effect*** among a meaningful number of footwear buyers. The loyalty effect is strongest for those that enjoy above-average market shares and thus are considered by buyers to have relatively attractive competitive offerings (based on price, quality, model selection, rebates, and so on). Recent studies of the behavior of athletic footwear buyers indicate that there is virtually no customer loyalty to company brands that are perceived as substantially over-priced or unfashionable or have otherwise less attractive attributes than rival brands. In other words, footwear buyers are more likely to be repeat-purchasers of those brands with leading market shares than of those brands that have sub-par market shares.

Competitive Strategy Options

With 11 competitive weapons at your disposal, you and your co-managers have many strategic options for positioning your company in the global marketplace and trying to out-compete rival companies. You can put more or less emphasis than competitors on winning sales in North America or Europe or Asia or Latin America. You can emphasize or de-emphasize private-label sales. In the branded market, you can pursue a competitive advantage keyed to low-cost/low-price, top-notch quality, brand name and brand image, a bigger network of retail outlets and retail megastores, a broader product line (up to 250 models), bigger promotional rebates, the convenience of online shopping, or any combination of these. You can pursue a similar competitive strategy in North America, Europe, Asia, and Latin America or you can craft different strategies keyed to the different conditions prevailing in each geographic market. ***There's no built-in bias that favors any one strategy over all the others.*** Most any well-conceived, well-executed competitive approach is capable of producing good financial performance, ***provided it is not overpowered by the strategies of your competitors***. Which company or companies win out in the upcoming battle for industry leadership will depend entirely on who is able to out-strategize, out-compete, and outperform the others.

The Demand Forecast Screen

To forecast the number of branded pairs your company can anticipate selling in each branded geographic region, you should go to the Menu Bar and select the Demand Forecast button, which will take you to the screen shown in Exhibit 3-2. There's a lot of information on the screen, so you will need to pay attention to the labels and calculations and give yourself time to absorb all that is happening on the screen. While the screen admittedly looks complicated, you'll find it is really pretty easy to use once you dig in, play around with some of the entries, make a couple of demand forecasts, and become familiar with how it works.

Exhibit 3-2

The Demand Forecast Screen

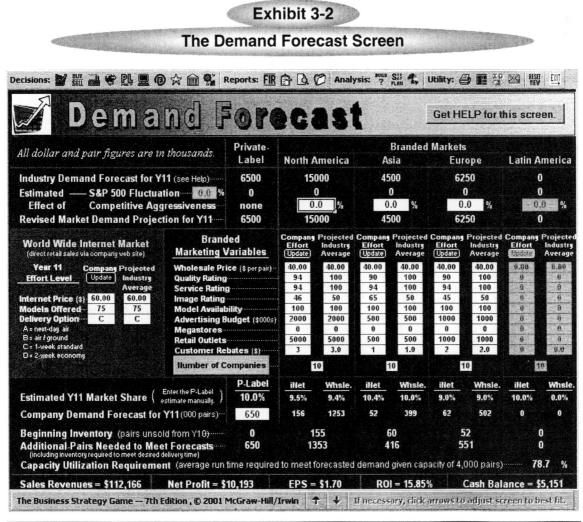

Adjusting for the S&P 500 and Competitive Aggressiveness. In the first block at the top of the screen are four rows of data and entries that allow you to "what-if" the effect of changes in the S&P 500 and above-average or below-average competitive aggressiveness. Keep in mind that year-to-year increases in the S&P 500 Index will boost footwear sales potentials worldwide whereas year-to-year declines will shrink worldwide market potential. ***The maximum impact is ±10%.*** The S&P 500 Index will have no impact on the Year 11 forecast, however. The S&P 500 Index value for Year 11 is the starting value; *the first impact of changes in the S&P 500 on forecasted sales potential comes in Year 12*. When your instructor/game administrator announces the new S&P Index value, you can calculate the percentage change and use it to *estimate* whether market demand is likely to be higher or lower than the unadjusted forecast provided in the Footwear Industry Report. For the first year of the simulation, you should enter 0 for each of the competitive aggressiveness fields. It will take several years for you to develop the data needed to analyze the effect of this adjustment factor.

Forecasting Your Company's Sales and Market Share. The middle block of data and entries on the Demand Forecast screen is the most important. On the left (light-shaded area in Exhibit 3-2), you should enter *tentative* values for the Internet price, the number of models offered, and speed of delivery option. Because online sales reach buyers across the world, it is company policy to offer a number of models online that is no greater than the smallest number of models available in any one of the company's regional warehouses.

Next you should proceed to enter *tentative* values for your company's branded sales effort—the numbers already on the screen are the values for the preceding year. The first column in each regional market merely records the current entries you've made on the branded marketing decisions screen (as concerns retail outlets, advertising, rebates, and wholesale selling price) and the other current factors that shape your company's overall competitive effort (number of models, product quality, customer service rating, and image rating) to win sales and market share in North America, Europe, Asia, and Latin America (the earliest you can begin selling in Latin America is Year 12). When you first arrive at the Demand Forecast screen, these same values already appear in the cells in the "what-if" marketing effort column (the second column). In the adjoining column (labeled Industry Average), you should enter your "best-guess" estimates of what the industry average competitive effort will be. In other words, your best estimate of the upcoming year's average selling price in the region, average quality rating in the region, average service rating in the region, and so on. This requires making judgments about whether competitors, on average, will increase/decrease their selling prices, product quality, service, number of models, advertising levels, and so forth. Then in the row below all these entries, you must enter how many companies you expect to be competing in the various geographic regions (in Year 11, it is likely, though not guaranteed, that all companies in the industry will compete for sales and market share in North America, Europe, and Asia). How many companies will actually go forward with plans to enter the Latin America market and begin selling branded footwear in Year 12 is, of course, highly uncertain and a potential source of error in your sales and market share forecast for that region. *The Company Demand Forecast values on the Demand Forecast screen include online sales in each geographic region of the world.*

The Importance of What-If. By "what-ifing" various values for your own company's selling price, quality, models, advertising, retail dealers, company-owned megastores, rebates, and so on, you can see the impact of various sales and marketing combinations on your company's *estimated* sales volume. You'll find "what-ifing" to be a critical ingredient of your decision-making process each year in arriving at a strategy for competing effectively against rivals and generating the revenues and sales volumes needed to produce good bottom-line performance.

In Year 11, for example, you know that branded footwear demand will *average* 1,500,000 pairs in North America, 450,000 pairs in Asia, and 625,000 pairs in Europe. By out-competing rival companies in a given geographic area, your company can achieve sales volumes exceeding these averages. *The demand forecasting screen is your best tool for judging what kind of sales and marketing effort your company will need to outsell rivals and to grow market share.* While taking some market share away from less competitive brands is very doable, the important thing to discover from what-ifing is what levels of pricing, product quality, advertising, and so on it will likely take to achieve sales volumes that are 20% to 30% or more above the market averages. The demand forecasting model will help you *estimate* the effect of a $1 lower selling price or a $2 million increase in advertising or a 15-point increase in quality on your company's sales volume. You'll find the estimates provided by the demand forecasting model to be much more reliable than guessing and hoping. If you and your co-managers want to be very aggressive and win enough market share away from rivals to outsell them by 50%, 75%, 100%, or more, the demand forecasting model can help you gauge what level of competitive effort it will take to achieve such results in the face of opposing competition from other companies (as represented by the industry average values that you and your co-managers anticipate will prevail). But you also have to understand that any market share gains your company achieves at the expense of rivals in one year may prove short-lived because rivals can be expected to retaliate in the following year by upping their competitive effort and trying to regain some of their market share losses.

What Can Cause the Demand Forecasts to be Wrong? The demand forecasting model provides you with only *projections* of your company's market share and how many pairs your company can expect to sell—the model's projections are not guarantees. The forecasted sales volumes and market shares may deviate from the actual sales and market shares for three reasons:

1. Your projections of one or more of the industry averages (and thus the degree of competition from rivals) may prove to be too high or too low.

2. The actual effect of changes in the S&P 500 Index or in the overall competitive aggressiveness of rivals can differ from your percentage estimates.

3. The number of companies competing in each geographic region may turn out to be more or less than you estimate.

Normally, the projected sales volumes will prove accurate within ±5% of the number of pairs actually sold, *provided your projections of the upcoming year's industry averages, the number of competitors in each geographic region, and the percentage changes in the S&P 500 and competitive aggressiveness are on target.*

Tips for Using the Demand Forecast Screen Effectively. The Demand Forecast screen provides you and your co-managers with a valuable tool for estimating the outcomes of different competitive effort combinations. If the projected market share and sales volumes are below the levels you would like (or if they exceed what you are able to produce and deliver), go back to the "company effort" column and watch what happens to the projected number of pairs sold when you raise/lower the number of models, increase/decrease quality, spend more/less on advertising, increase/decrease the wholesale price, and so on. By playing around with different combinations of prices, models, quality, rebates, advertising, and so on, you can get a pretty good handle on what combination of competitive effort is likely to be needed to achieve the desired market share and sales volume in each of the three branded markets. When you and your co-managers reach a consensus on the what-if entries for your company (models, quality, retail outlets, rebates, advertising, and so on) that you believe will be needed to achieve the desired sales volumes and market shares, *given the anticipated competition from rivals that are reflected in the industry averages you have entered*, then you are ready to move to the production and warehousing and shipping screens and make decisions to stock the various distribution warehouses with the necessary pairs to meet the associated sales and inventory requirements.

In the years ahead, you'll find that the Demand Forecast screen provides valuable guidance in forecasting sales and in helping you and your co-managers choose what price to charge and what branded marketing effort to employ. To make the most effective use of the Demand Forecast Screen, do the following:

- *Go to the Demand Forecast screen early in your decision-making process to develop a rough or preliminary company demand forecast as a starting point for planning how many pairs to produce at your plants and how many pairs to ship to each of the distribution warehouses*. Once you have a tentative idea of how many pairs you can expect to sell in the upcoming year, you can quickly move on to the decision screens for plant operations, warehousing and shipping, and marketing operations and make decisions in all of the areas as required. As you and your co-managers decide what to do in all these areas of the company's operations, you can track the impact on sales revenues, net profit, EPS, ROI, and Cash by monitoring the last row of calculations at the bottom of the screen— these are updated each time you enter a new decision. When you have made a complete trial decision, return to the Demand Forecasting screen to revise and refine your sales forecast. You can press the Update button to automatically import all the branded marketing decisions on the decision screens back into your demand forecast. If you are not satisfied with the projected outcomes for revenues, net profit, EPS, ROI, and cash balance at the bottom of the screen or if you want to explore ways to boost overall company performance, then do some what-ifing.

- *Use the Demand Forecast screen to "what-if" the impact of competitors' actions on your company's sales and market share*. Competitors might, for instance, decide to trim their selling prices, pushing the industry average in North America down from $40 to $38. To see what such a change would do to your company's sales volume in North America, simply change the projected industry average wholesale price for North America from $40 to $38 and see what happens to your forecasted volume and percentage share. You can play around with different values for the various industry averages to get a good feel for the downside risks in your sales and market share forecasts should rivals unexpectedly increase their competitive effort. If you and your co-managers are in doubt about what industry average values to use as the basis for your demand forecast, then one good approach is to run worst-case and best-case scenarios. The worst-case scenario entails entering fairly strong increases in the industry averages (which signals stronger competition in the marketplace than previously) and observing the resulting downside impact on your projected sales volumes and market share. A best-case scenario involves entering little or no increase in the industry averages (which signals not much change in rivals' overall competitive effort) and observing the upside impact on your company's projected sales volumes and market shares. The worst-case and best-case projections provide a *range* in which your actual sales volumes and market shares should fall.

- *Use the Demand Forecast screen to "what-if" the changes in your own company's sales volumes and market shares should you increase or decrease your competitive effort.* For instance, you can "what-if" the impact of increasing your price in Europe from $40 to $42.50. The calculations on the screen will show you what the projected decline in unit sales and market share will be and, even more important, what the impact would be on company revenues, net profits, EPS, ROI, and cash balance (the last row at the bottom of the screen). In similar fashion, you can try changing other elements of your company's competitive effort—product quality, rebates, advertising, or dealer service—to see what the impact would be on forecasted sales, market share, revenues, net profit, EPS, and so on. This will help you zero in on what decision combination will produce the overall best set of results.

In the event you experience difficulty in generating relatively accurate forecasts of unit sales and market shares, it is nearly always because of having significantly misjudged the upcoming year's industry averages for several of the competitive variables. To correct this, you'll need to spend more time and effort studying what rival companies are doing, using the information provided in the Footwear Industry Report and the Competitor Analysis Report as a basis for your analysis. Keep in mind, most all companies are not going to utilize the same competitive effort in the upcoming year as they did last year. Just as you and your co-managers will decide to increase or decrease prices, quality, rebates, advertising, and so on to improve your company's market share and performance, the managers of rival companies are likely to make changes in their overall competitive effort to enhance their company's performance. Companies that did poorly in the last year are strong candidates to make significant changes, and the industry leaders, despite having performed well, may institute significant changes as well in order to remain in the lead. Hence there are strong reasons for expecting some kind of change in the industry averages, as opposed to assuming last year's averages will remain largely unchanged. It is up to you and your co-managers to be astute "market-watchers" and "competitor-watchers"; by Year 14 or 15, you'll have enough data points for each of the industry averages to spot trends and you'll begin to get a feel for how competitive market conditions are changing.

Plant Operations

Plant operations is one of the most strategically and operationally important areas of the company. Currently, the company has two plants, a 1 million-pair North American plant near San Antonio, Texas, and a recently constructed 3 million-pair plant in Asia. Given the expected growth in the global demand for athletic footwear, it is likely that you will find it desirable to construct additional production capacity—by expanding the existing plants and/or building new plants in Europe or Latin America or both. You may also elect to buy plant capacity from other companies in the industry or sell all or part of your existing plant capacity to interested rivals. Putting together a profitable production strategy for your company and operating the company's plants in a cost-effective manner will thus occupy the time of you and your co-managers each decision period.

The latest company report on your company's manufacturing operations is shown in Exhibit 4-1. *All figures in this and other company reports are in thousands, except for the percentages and per pair items.* The Manufacturing Report, provided annually after each year's decisions are processed, gives you a rundown of production operations: manufacturing costs, assorted manufacturing statistics, the amount invested in plant and equipment, and plant capacity information. All the zeros in the columns for Europe and Latin America reflect the fact that your company has not yet built plants in these regions of the world.

Exhibit 4-1

The Manufacturing Report

	N. AMERICA		ASIA		EUROPE		L. AMERICA		
	P-Label	Branded	P-Label	Branded	P-Label	Branded	P-Label	Branded	OVERALL
MANUFACTURING COSTS ($000s)									
Materials —— Normal-Wear	0	4,320	2,300	8,500	0	0	0	0	15,120
Long-Wear	0	2,400	1,278	4,722	0	0	0	0	8,400
Labor ——— Annual Wages	0	4,000	511	1,889	0	0	0	0	6,400
Incentive Pay	0	570	132	486	0	0	0	0	1,188
Overtime Pay	0	0	0	0	0	0	0	0	0
Plant Supervision	0	1,200	341	1,259	0	0	0	0	2,800
Quality Control	0	640	341	1,259	0	0	0	0	2,240
Styling / Features	0	1,000	200	600	0	0	0	0	1,800
Methods Improvements	0	0	0	0	0	0	0	0	0
Production Run Set-Up	0	2,000	1,000	1,000	0	0	0	0	4,000
Plant Maintenance	0	2,150	1,491	5,509	0	0	0	0	9,150
Depreciation	0	1,000	746	2,755	0	0	0	0	4,501
Total Manufacturing Cost	0	19,280	8,340	27,979	0	0	0	0	55,599
MANUFACTURING STATISTICS									
Specifications —— Quality	0	100	75	100	0	0	0	0	
Models	0	100	100	100	0	0	0	0	
Pairs Produced (000s)	0	800	426	1,574	0	0	0	0	2,800
Pairs Rejected (000s)	0	40	26	102	0	0	0	0	168
Net Production (000s)	0	760	400	1,472	0	0	0	0	2,632
Reject Rate (%)	0.00	5.00	5.50	6.50	0.00	0.00	0.00	0.00	6.00
Avg. Quality Control ($ / pair prod.)	0.80		0.80		0.00		0.00		
Avg. Methods Imp. ($ / pair capacity)	0.00		0.00		0.00		0.00		
Worker Productivity —— Year 10	4,000		2,500		0		0		
(pairs / worker / year) Last Yr.	4,000		2,500		0		0		
LABOR STATISTICS									
Number of ——— Beginning	200		800		0		0		1,000
Employees Hired (Fired)	0		0		0		0		0
Current	200		800		0		0		1,000
Compensation — Annual Wage	20.0		3.0		0.0		0.0		6.4
($000s per Incentive Pay	2.1		0.8		0.0		0.0		1.1
employee) Total	22.1		3.8		0.0		0.0		7.5
PLANT INVESTMENT ($000s)									
Beginning Net Investment	16,000		66,500		0		0		82,500
Plus Capital Additions	0		0		0		0		0
Less Y10 Depreciation	1,000		3,500		0		0		4,500
Ending Net Investment	15,000		63,000		0		0		78,000
CAPACITY STATISTICS (000s)									
Year 10 Plant Capacity	1,000		3,000		0		0		4,000
New Plant Construction	0		0		0		0		0
Plant Capacity Expansion	0		0		0		0		0
Plant Capacity for Year 11	1,000		3,000		0		0		4,000
Max. Production (at full OT)	1,200		2,400		0		0		3,600
Automation of ——·Option A	-----		-----		-----		-----		
Plants Option B	-----		-----		-----		-----		
(year ordered) Option C	-----		-----		-----		-----		
Option D	-----		-----		-----		-----		
Option E	-----		-----		-----		-----		
Option F	-----		-----		-----		-----		

There are several things worth mentioning about the manufacturing report in Exhibit 4-1 and about your company's production operations:

- Materials costs in Year 10 were lower that the *base* material prices of $9 per pair for normal-wear and $15 per pair for long-wear. This is because industry-wide capacity utilization in Year 10 was 70%—as stated in Section 1, whenever worldwide shoe production falls below 90% of the footwear industry's worldwide plant capacity, the market prices for both normal and long-wear materials drop 1% for each 1% below the 90% capacity utilization level. The company maintains no inventories of normal-wear and long-wear materials because suppliers have the capability to make deliveries on an as-needed basis. Plant managers provide suppliers with production schedules two weeks in advance to enable them to arrange for materials deliveries.

- Labor costs consist of base wages and fringe benefits, piecework incentives paid for each pair produced that meet quality standards, and overtime pay. In Year 10, labor costs totaled $4,570,000 at the North American plant and $3,018,000 at the Asian plant. Given production of 800,000 pairs in North America and 2,000,000 pairs in Asia, this is equivalent to labor costs per pair produced of $5.71 in Ohio ($4,570,000 ÷ 800,000 pairs = $5.7125) and $1.51 in Asia ($3,018,000 ÷ 2,000,000 pairs = $1.509). The per pair labor cost differential between the two plants stemmed from differing wage rates ($20,000 versus $3,000), incentive pay ($2,100 versus $800), and productivity levels (4,000 pairs per worker versus 2,500). The sizable labor cost differential between the two plants should be a matter of concern and is something you and your co-managers ought to address in the upcoming years.

- *All overtime work in all geographic areas entails overtime labor costs equal to 1.5 times the normal base wage cost per pair produced*; the prevailing piecework incentive bonus is also paid on all non-defective pairs produced at overtime in addition to the overtime wage. Although there was no use of overtime in Year 10, any future amounts for overtime pay that are reported will always include *all* overtime compensation—overtime wages plus the applicable incentive pay per pair at overtime. *The number of pairs which can be produced at a plant without the use of overtime is limited to plant capacity or to the number of workers employed times productivity per worker, whichever is less.* For instance, if you and your co-managers decide next year to employ 700 workers at the Asian plant (instead of 800 as in Year 10), and if worker productivity continues to be 2,500 pairs per worker per year, then the maximum number of pairs which can be produced without use of overtime is 700 × 2,500 or 1,750,000 pairs; with a workforce of 700 and productivity of 2,500 pairs, overtime production will thus begin at 1,750,000 pairs instead of 3,000,000 pairs. Moreover, the maximum amount that can be produced at overtime with 700 workers is 20% of 1,750,000 pairs or 350,000 pairs, not 400,000 pairs as would be the case if the plant were staffed to full production capacity with 800 workers.

- The amount spent on quality control is important in two respects: First, annual expenditure on QC at a given plant has a significant impact on the number of pairs that pass final inspection. The bigger the annual QC effort at a plant (measured in terms of QC expenditures per pair produced), the smaller the reject rate at final inspection. Second, the annual quality control expenditures at a plant and the cumulative quality control expenditures per pair produced companywide are two of the major components in the International Footwear Federation's annual quality rating calculation.

- The company maintains a staff of people who work exclusively on keeping the company's product line fresh and innovative. Once management decides how many models to produce at each plant (the options are 50, 100, 150, 200, or 250), this staff is charged with coming up with the needed footwear designs and styling/features for the company to promote each year. The caliber of their styles and designs is a function of the size budget they are given; the amount budgeted per model/style at each plant is used by the International Footwear Federation in calculating the plant's annual quality rating.

- Production run set-up costs vary according to the number of models produced at a plant. The annual set-up cost for 50 models is $1 million per plant; for 100 models it is $2 million per plant; for 150 models it is $4 million per plant, for 200 models it is $6.5 million per plant, and for 250 models it is $9 million. The size of the plant does not matter in determining production run set-up costs, only the number of models. Both the North American and Asian plants produced 100 models/styles of athletic footwear in Year 10.

- Maintenance costs in a given year equal 5% of gross plant investment plus another 0.25% for each year of age past five years. "Gross plant investment" represents the total dollar amounts the company has invested in each plant (initial plant costs, the capital cost associated with any expansion, plus any investment in plant upgrades). This amount is not shown on the report but is nonetheless accurately tracked by company accountants.

- Plant life is 20 years, and depreciation is calculated on a straight-line basis equal to 5% of gross plant investment per year.

- Worker productivity at each plant is affected by five things: (1) the **percentage** increase in the annual wage granted to workers each year, (2) how much emphasis is placed on incentive compensation (as measured by the percentage of the company's total compensation package accounted for by incentive pay), (3) how the company's total compensation package (annual wage plus total incentive pay before any overtime) compares against the average compensation package of other footwear companies with plants in the same geographic area, (4) whether you are expanding employment and hiring additional workers or cutting employment levels by laying off workers, and (5) your expenditures for production methods improvements in each plant.

- Net plant investment represents the undepreciated book value of the plant—in accounting terms, it equals gross plant investment less accumulated depreciation.

As the simulation progresses, you will have opportunities to improve the operating efficiency of your plants and lower costs. Company co-managers can take any of several actions to operate the company's plants more effectively and efficiently:

- Undertaking any of six capital improvement projects to upgrade plant operations.

- Increasing annual efforts to improve production methods.

- Altering annual wages and piecework incentives in ways that boost the productivity of the plant workforce.

- Taking actions to lower the number and percentage of defective pairs produced (Year 10 reject rates were 5.4% at the North American plant and 5.7% at the Asian plant).

Exhibit 4-2 shows itemized Year 10 production costs by plant and by type product for the company's two plants. You will be provided with copies of both reports after each year's decisions have been processed as a basis for analyzing and improving your company's plant operations.

Exhibit 4-2

Production Costs by Plant and by Product

	N. AMERICA		ASIA		EUROPE		L. AMERICA		OVERALL
	P-Label	Branded	P-Label	Branded	P-Label	Branded	P-Label	Branded	
Materials —–Normal-Wear	0.00	5.40	5.40	5.40	0.00	0.00	0.00	0.00	5.40
Long-Wear	0.00	3.00	3.00	3.00	0.00	0.00	0.00	0.00	3.00
Total	0.00	8.40	8.40	8.40	0.00	0.00	0.00	0.00	8.40
Labor ——— Annual Wages	0.00	5.00	1.20	1.20	0.00	0.00	0.00	0.00	2.29
Incentive Pay	0.00	0.71	0.31	0.31	0.00	0.00	0.00	0.00	0.42
Overtime Pay	0.00	0.00	0.00	0.00	0.00	0.00	0.00	0.00	0.00
Total	0.00	5.71	1.51	1.51	0.00	0.00	0.00	0.00	2.71
Plant Supervision	0.00	1.50	0.80	0.80	0.00	0.00	0.00	0.00	1.00
Quality Control	0.00	0.80	0.80	0.80	0.00	0.00	0.00	0.00	0.80
Styling / Features	0.00	1.25	0.47	0.38	0.00	0.00	0.00	0.00	0.64
Production Methods	0.00	0.00	0.00	0.00	0.00	0.00	0.00	0.00	0.00
Waste due to Rejects	0.00	1.27	1.27	1.23	0.00	0.00	0.00	0.00	1.27
Production Run Set-Up	0.00	2.50	2.35	0.64	0.00	0.00	0.00	0.00	1.43
Plant Maintenance	0.00	2.69	3.50	3.50	0.00	0.00	0.00	0.00	3.27
Depreciation	0.00	1.25	1.75	1.75	0.00	0.00	0.00	0.00	1.61
Total Cost Per Pair Produced	0.00	25.37	20.85	19.01	0.00	0.00	0.00	0.00	21.12

(adjusted for rejects)

Pertinent Production Issues

One production issue is how many private-label pairs to produce versus how many branded pairs to produce and at which plants to produce them. Prior management opted to make all private-label footwear at the Asian plant because of the significantly lower labor costs in Asia. Keeping production costs on private-label footwear as low as possible was deemed essential because of the lower price at which private label shoes are sold—$40 per pair for branded shoes versus $34 per pair for private label footwear in Year 10. Despite the lower price, private label sales have been an attractive distribution channel, generating Year 10 profits for the company of more than $2 million. Continuing to participate in the private-label segment, in the short run at least, would seem prudent. Prior management was unsure whether to pursue branded sales in all four geographic markets or to focus on building market-leading positions in just one or two geographic markets. While the earliest you can begin selling in Latin America is Year 12 (plans and arrangements for warehousing and shipping will not be finalized until the end of Year 11), the decision of how many branded pairs to produce will be driven partly by which branded markets you and you co-managers elect to focus on and the market share targets you wish to achieve. Related to the issue of branded shoe production is the quality of the branded footwear you wish to make. Prior management was unsure whether the company should produce essentially the same quality branded shoes for all branded market segments or whether to make high-quality shoes for some markets and low-quality shoes for others. You and your co-managers will have the latitude to pursue a low-cost/low-price strategy in one branded market arena and a high quality/premium price/strong brand image strategy in another geographic region should you choose to do so.

A second, production issue is where to locate additional production capacity. A European plant is economically attractive because of the potential distribution cost savings (tariff avoidance and lower shipping costs) on future sales made in Europe; plant sites in Spain or Italy offer ample labor supplies and reasonable wage costs. A Latin American plant is economically attractive partly because of potential distribution cost savings on future sales in Latin America but mainly because of very low wage rates and the ready availability of both labor and plant sites; any pairs not sold in Latin America can be exported to other geographic markets. A large-scale Asian plant could become the company's principal production site, with pairs being exported to Europe and North America to meet growing demand in those markets. Having plants in all four geographic areas avoids the cost problems of tariff barriers but there can be economy-of-scale advantages to having one or two large plants as opposed to three or four smaller plants. You'll have to decide what sort of plant configuration best fits your strategy.

Third and last, you and your co-managers need to address (1) whether to initiate plant upgrades or make other operating changes so as to reduce the relatively high labor costs at the company's plant in North America and (2) whether to make base pay and incentive compensation adjustments at the North American and Asian plants in Year 11.

You can take decisive action to resolve all of these issues quickly or adopt a cautious "wait-and-see" posture and defer actions until later.

Production and Labor Decisions

Each decision period you and your co-managers must make a series of decisions concerning plant operations and footwear production. All the decisions made each year are shown on the upper portion of the manufacturing decisions screen (the light-shaded area in Exhibit 4-3). The numbers appearing in the boxed decision entry cells represent prior management's decisions for Year 10. The information appearing in the lower portion of the screen represents calculations instantaneously provided by the computer each time you make a decision entry or a what-if entry (these numbers are *projections* of the upcoming year's results based on the decision entries currently residing on *all 10 decision screens*). These calculations will help you assess the economics of the various decision options and give you a stronger basis for deciding what to do.

There will be no S&P 500 or exchange rate impacts in Year 11. Changes in these rates will first come into play in Year 12.

How Many Pairs to Produce. The three biggest factors to consider in deciding how many pairs to produce are (1) the number of pairs in inventory in each distribution center that went unsold in Year 10, (2) how many branded pairs you want left in inventory at the end of Year 11 as a safety buffer against stockouts or as a deliberate inventory build up to support sales in future years, and (3) how many private-label and branded pairs you expect to sell in Year 11—as determined by the entries you made on the Demand Forecast screen (discussed in Section 2). As was indicated earlier, the footwear demand forecasts for Years 11 and 12 are as follows:

	Private-Label Demand (in pairs)	Branded Demand (in pairs)				Worldwide Demand (in pairs)
		North America	Asia	Europe	Latin America	
Year 11	650,000	1,500,000	450,000	625,000	---	3.225,000
Year 12	700,000	1,650,000	575,000	725,000	300,000	3,950,000

These are ***averages per company***. Your company's sales in an area can be more or less than the average, according to whether your company's competitive effort is stronger or weaker than the efforts expended by rival companies.

Exhibit 4-3

Production and Labor Decision Screen

	N. A. Plant		Asian Plant		European Plant		L. A. Plant	
Total footwear production needed (after rejects) to meet demand forecast and delivery time inventory requirements. Private-Label: 650 Branded: 2,320	1000 pairs, 1200 at max OT		3000 pairs, 3600 at max OT		0 pairs, 0 at max OT		0 pairs, 0 at max OT	
	P-Label	Branded	P-Label	Branded	P-Label	Branded	P-Label	Branded
Pairs To Be Manufactured (000s of pairs)	0	800	423	1574	0	0	0	0
Long-Wear Materials Usage (0-100%)	0	25 %	25	25 %	0	0 %	0	0 %
Number of Models (50, 100, 150, 200, 250)	0	100	100	100	0	0	0	0
Styling and Features Budget ($000s)	$ 0	1000	$ 200	600	$ 0	0	$ 0	0
General Budgets — Quality Control	$ 640		$ 1600		$ 0		$ 0	
($000s) Methods Improvements	$ 0		$ 0		$ 0		$ 0	
Compensation — Annual Wage (000s of $)	$ 20.0 Incentive		$ 3.0 Incentive		$ 0.0 Incentive		$ 0.0 Incentive	
Incentive Pay ($ per pair)	$ 0.75	13.0%	$ 0.33	21.6%	$ 0.00	0.0%	$ 0.00	0.0%
Productivity Estimate for Y11 (actual for Y10)	4044	(4000)	2527	(2500)	0	(0)	0	(0)
Workers Needed (maximum / minimum at full OT)	198 / 165		791 / 659		0 / 0		0 / 0	
Total Number of Workers Employed	200		800		0		0	
Workers Hired (Laid Off) in Year 11	0		0		0		0	

Production Statistics	P-Label	Branded	P-Label	Branded	P-Label	Branded	P-Label	Branded
Quality Rating of Pairs Produced	0	100	78	90	0	0	0	0
Estimated Reject Rate (accurate to within ±0.5%)	0.00	5.33 %	5.71	5.71 %	0.00	0.00 %	0.00	0.00 %
Net Production (000s of pairs after rejects)	0	757	399	1484	0	0	0	0
Materials	0.00	9.45	9.45	9.45	0.00	0.00	0.00	0.00
Materials Price Variable Labor — Regular	0.00	5.71	1.51	1.51	0.00	0.00	0.00	0.00
Estimates Y11 Manufact. Overtime	0.00	0.00	0.00	0.00	0.00	0.00	0.00	0.00
Normal-Wear Costs Plant Supervision	0.00	1.50	0.80	0.80	0.00	0.00	0.00	0.00
$8.10 All Other	0.00	3.48	2.52	2.32	0.00	0.00	0.00	0.00
Long-Wear Fixed Mfg. Production Run Set-Up	0.00	2.50	2.36	0.64	0.00	0.00	0.00	0.00
$13.50 Costs Maint. & Depreciation	0.00	4.00	5.26	5.26	0.00	0.00	0.00	0.00
Total Manufacturing Cost ($ per pair)	0.00	26.64	21.90	19.98	0.00	0.00	0.00	0.00

Sales Revenues = $112,166	Net Profit = $10,193	EPS = $1.70	ROI = 15.85%	Cash Balance = $5,151

The Business Strategy Game — 7th Edition, © 2001 McGraw-Hill/Irwin   ↑ ↓   If necessary, click arrows to adjust screen to best fit.

With maximum use of overtime, your company has the manufacturing capacity to produce as many as 1,200,000 pairs at the North American plant and as many as 3,600,000 pairs at the Asian plant. You will need to decide how many branded and private-label pairs to produce at each plant. Prior management elected to make all private-label shoes in Asia because the lower labor costs at the Asian plant provided a bigger profit margin on private-label sales.

Materials Decisions. All of the materials used in producing athletic footwear are readily available on the open market. Some 300 suppliers worldwide have the capability to furnish interior lining fabrics, waterproof fabrics and plastics for external use, rubber and plastic materials for soles, shoelaces, and high-strength thread. It is substantially cheaper for footwear manufacturers to purchase these materials from outside suppliers than it is to manufacture them internally in the relatively small volumes needed. Delivery time on all materials is no more than 48 hours, allowing manufacturers to operate on a just-in-time delivery basis.

Suppliers offer two basic grades of raw materials: normal-wear and long-wear. Long-wear fabrics and shoe sole materials improve shoe quality and performance, but they currently cost two-thirds more than normal-wear components. Materials for a shoe made completely of long-wear components cost $15 per pair versus a cost of $9 per pair for shoes made entirely of normal-wear components. However, *shoes can be manufactured with any percentage combination of normal-wear and long-wear materials*. All footwear-making equipment in present and future plants permits use of a mixture of normal-wear and long-wear components.

All materials suppliers charge the going market price, and the qualities of long-wear and normal-wear materials are the same from supplier to supplier. Materials prices fluctuate according to worldwide supply-demand conditions. *Whenever worldwide shoe production falls below 90% of the footwear industry's worldwide plant capacity (not counting overtime production capability), the market prices for both normal and long-wear materials drop 1% for each 1% below the 90% capacity utilization level.* Such price reductions reflect weak demand and increased competition among materials suppliers for the available orders. Conversely, *whenever worldwide shoe production exceeds 100% of worldwide plant capacity utilization (meaning that companies, on average, are producing at overtime), the market prices for normal and long-wear materials rise 1% for each 1% that worldwide capacity utilization exceeds 100%.* Such price increases reflect strong demand for materials and greater ability on the part of suppliers to get away with charging more for essential raw materials.

Materials prices fluctuate according to worldwide utilization of footwear plant capacity and the percentage use of long-wear materials.

A second demand-supply condition causing materials prices to change is widespread substitution of long-wear materials for normal-wear materials. *Once global usage of long-wear materials passes the 25% level, the prices of long-wear materials rise 0.5% for each 1% that the percentage use of long-wear materials exceeds 25%; simultaneously, the worldwide market price of normal-wear materials will fall 0.5% for each 1% that the global usage of normal-wear materials falls below 75%.* Thus the price gap between long-wear and normal-wear materials widens as global use of long-wear materials rises above 25%.

Materials prices in Year 10 were $7.20 for normal-wear and $12.00 for long-wear because capacity utilization in Year 10 was 70% (20% below the 90% threshold). The Materials Price Estimates box on the lower left side of Exhibit 4-3 shows the expected materials prices for the upcoming year based on (1) a rough estimate of the industry-wide capacity utilization needed to meet projected demand in the upcoming year, (2) global long-wear materials usage in the previous year, and (3) company expenditures on production methods improvements. These estimated materials prices are used to calculate projected materials costs for the upcoming year. *When the upcoming year's results are processed, the materials prices you actually incur may be higher or lower than the estimates provided on the Production and Labor Screen*, because actual industry-wide capacity utilization and long-wear materials usage may differ from what was estimated.

Despite price fluctuations, materials suppliers have ample capacity to furnish whatever volume of materials that manufacturers need. No shortages have occurred in the past. Just recently, suppliers indicated they would have no difficulty in accommodating increased materials demand in the event footwear-makers build additional plant capacity to meet the growing demand for athletic-style shoes. *Footwear manufacturers are thus assured of receiving all orders for normal-wear and long-wear materials* no matter how much new footwear capacity is built down the road.

The only materials-related decisions you make concern the percentage mix of long-wear and normal-wear materials to be used in producing private-label and branded footwear at each plant; "the computer" will automatically take care of ordering the needed amount of materials based on the number of pairs you and your co-managers decide to produce. You can use the *same* normal-wear/long-wear mix to make private label and branded footwear (as in Year 10 at the Asian plant) or you can use *different* percentage mixes. Moreover, *you have the flexibility to vary the mix of normal-wear and long-wear materials from plant to plant*, thus allowing the company to produce private-label and branded shoes of varying quality at different plants. Producing different quality branded shoes at different plants can be beneficial if you and your co-managers wish to sell different quality branded footwear in different geographic markets.

Assuming no change in the other quality-determining factors, an increase in the long-wear materials percentage will boost the quality of a plant's output and a decrease will lower it. The International Footwear Federation's product quality formula is programmed in so that you can immediately see the impact on product quality of a change in the percentage use of long-wear materials—quality rating projections appear on the first line of Production Statistics section in Exhibit 4-3. Also, you will be able to see the cost impact of raising/lowering the long-wear materials mix by watching the changes in materials cost and manufacturing cost per pair produced (in the lower portion of the screen) as you make different entries for the long-wear percentage.

Decisions Regarding the Number of Models. You and your co-managers have the option at each plant of producing 50, 100, 150, 200, or 250 models. Production run set-up costs at each plant are $1 million for making 50 models; $2 million for 100 models; $4 million for 150 models; $6.5 million for 200 models; and $9 million for 250 models. Widening your company's product line to include more models can have a strongly positive effect on unit sales and market share. But the sales-enhancing effect of more models also carries a potentially sizable impact on *per pair* production costs. At the North American plant, for example, producing 1 million pairs and 50 models entails production run set-up costs of $1.00 per pair whereas producing 1 million pairs and 250 models entails set-up costs of $9.00 per pair. At the bigger Asian plant, however, producing 3 million pairs and 250 models results in set-up costs of just $3.00 per pair. If a major element of your company's strategy is to have a broad product line, you can combat the added cost per pair associated with production run set-up costs by initiating a plant upgrade to cut these costs (see option F in Exhibit 4-5 discussed later in this section). Producing more models at each plant also affects the number of defective pairs. *The more models produced, the higher the reject rate*; this is because more frequent production run changeovers result in reduced worker experience and skill in making each model. Furthermore, increasing the number of models produced will lower the quality rating; this is because the quality rating is partly a function of the amount spent for styling and features *per model*. You can overcome the erosion of the quality rating by increasing expenditures for styling/features (or by increasing quality control expenditures or by using a larger percentage of long-wear materials, as discussed below).

> The wider the selection of models/styles offered, the wider the appeal of your product line, but unless corrective measures are taken, more models will increase reject rates and decrease quality ratings.

It is important to understand that producing 100 models in the North American plant and 100 models in the Asian plant entails producing the *same* set of 100 models at each plant, *not* entirely different sets of models/styles. When footwear from different plants producing different numbers of models/styles is shipped to a particular distribution warehouse (Memphis, Brussels, or Singapore), the resulting number of models/styles available to buyers in the market served by that warehouse equals the weighted average number of models. For example, if the North American plant produces 1 million pairs and 50 models and the Asian plant produces 3 million pairs and 100 models and if 400,000 pairs from each plant are then shipped to the Brussels warehouse, model availability in Europe will be an average of 75 models/styles (assuming no inventory of pairs in Brussels). If there are already some pairs in inventory in Brussels, the 75-model average will be adjusted up or down based on the number of models in inventory.

The number of models your company makes available in each geographic market is *a big driver* of your company's branded sales and market share. The wider the selection of models/styles offered (shoes for men, women, and children, and styles suitable for running, jogging, aerobics, basketball, tennis, golf, casual wear, etc.), the wider the appeal of your product line. *Other things being equal (price, quality, brand image, service, and so on), companies with a bigger selection of models in a particular geographic region will outsell companies with a smaller selection.*

Decisions Regarding Styling/Features and Quality Control. How much you and your co-managers decide to spend for styling/features per model and for quality control at each plant affect the International Footwear Federation's ratings of product quality at each plant. As you make entries for models, styling/features, and quality control, the computer uses the International Footwear Federation's quality rating formula to calculate product quality at each plant—see the first line in the Production Statistics section on the screen in Exhibit 4-3. You can enter different values for models, styling/features, and quality control, until you are satisfied with the resulting quality of branded and private-label footwear being produced and the production cost per pair. Because the quality of footwear produced at one plant is affected by the company's overall cumulative quality control effort, it is possible for increases or decreases in quality control spending at one plant to spill over to affect the quality of footwear output at another plant.

The four factors that determine product quality are:

1. Long-wear materials percentage
2. Quality control expenditures per pair produced (in the current year)
3. Cumulative quality control expenditures per pair produced
4. Styling/features budget per model

Decisions Regarding Production Methods Improvement. This decision option allows you to budget dollars for continuous improvements in work practices and plant efficiency. These expenditures go for worker training and skills development and to cover the costs of altering plant layouts and production procedures to achieve efficiency gains. *The money you spend at a particular plant for methods improvements acts to (1) reduce materials costs at the plant by as much as 25%, (2) reduce supervision costs in the plant by as much as 25%, and (3) increase worker productivity by as much as 10%.* However, the full benefits cannot be reached in a single year—it will take a sustained spending effort over 5 years or more to approach the maximum gains. Expenditures for improved production methods have the same impact in all plants. In Year 10, the company spent $23,520,000 on footwear materials and $2,800,000 on plant supervision costs, so a 25% annual savings could prove significant. A 10% increase in worker productivity in North America where productivity is presently

Expenditures for production methods improvements in a particular plant act to:

• Reduce materials costs.
• Reduce plant supervision costs.
• Increase worker productivity.

4,000 pairs per worker per year and in Asia where productivity is presently 2,500 pairs per worker per year also holds potential for meaningful cost reductions.

The size of the cost reductions for materials costs and plant supervision are a function of the *average annual amount spent per pair of production capacity*; the size of the gains in productivity are a function of *annual expenditures per plant employee*. Because the benefits your company will realize from expenditures on production methods improvement associated with materials costs and plant supervision costs depend on the *average annual* amount spent per pair of production capacity, you should view such expenditures as part of an ongoing effort to drive costs down rather than as something to be done intermittently. For example, if you spend $1.00 per pair on production methods improvement in Year 11 and $0 per pair in Year 12, the annual average drops to $0.50 in Year 12 and some of the benefits gained in Year 11 will erode from a lack of effort in Year 12. Likewise, a plant expansion will reduce the average amount spent per pair unless total spending for methods improvements is increased in proportion to production capacity. Also, you'll find there are diminishing marginal benefits to spending additional sums for production methods improvement—the incremental benefits from increasing spending from the equivalent of $0.50 per pair to $1.00 per pair of capacity will exceed the benefits associated with increasing spending from $1.00 to $1.50 per pair; and so on.

You can readily check out the benefits versus the costs of making expenditures for production methods improvements by observing the estimated effect on labor productivity (line 3 in the compensation section) and by monitoring the estimated impacts on materials costs, labor costs, plant supervision costs, and overall manufacturing costs per pair each time you enter a different level of expenditure for production methods improvement. By comparing the benefits and costs of several "what-if" entries for production methods expenditures, you'll be able to hone in on what benefits you can capture from various levels of production methods expenditure in any one year. As mentioned above, however, you will have to make production methods expenditures every year to approach realize the s most economic.

Compensation Decisions. Your and your co-managers must make two compensation decisions each year: (1) whether and how much to change the annual wage paid to plant workers and (2) whether and how much to change incentive pay. The compensation decisions made by prior management in Year 10 are shown in Exhibit 4-3. The company's Human Resource Department has done careful analysis over the years to determine how productivity responds to the various compensation options. Exhibit 4-4 summarizes HR's findings. These findings have been incorporated into the productivity estimate calculations (line 3 of the compensation decision section of the production and labor decisions screen in Exhibit 4-3). You can observe the estimated impact of the compensation decisions entered by watching what happens to estimated worker productivity and by looking at the effect on labor costs per pair produced in the manufacturing cost calculations section; these estimates will help you judge whether to change or stick with the decision entry. You'll find it relatively easy to "what-if" a variety of different compensation packages to arrive at one you deem attractive from a productivity-enhancing standpoint and affordable from a cost perspective.

The minimum annual wage for North America is $18,000; in Europe the minimum is $12,000, and in Asia and Latin America it is $2,500—unless otherwise announced.

In deciding upon the annual wage, you can grant a wage increase, leave the wage as is, or institute a wage cut. The annual wage amount is entered in thousands—a wage of $22,400 is entered as 22.4; a wage of $3,100 is entered as 3.1.

Exhibit 4-4

Factors That Affect Work Force Productivity

Compensation Factors	Impact	Comments
Bigger percent increases in annual wage	The greater the percentage increase in the annual wage, the greater the positive impact on workforce productivity. Annual wage increases in the 5-10% range can lead to productivity gains of as much as 6%. As the size of the annual wage increase approaches 12% in any one year, the productivity gains flatten out.	The projected productivity gain associated with raising the annual base wage is indicated in the calculations sections of the production and labor decisions screen each time you make an entry for the annual wage.
Zero increases in the annual wage and cuts in the annual wage	Cutting or even failing to increase the annual wage can have a negative impact on worker productivity, but can be partially offset with: • Attractive incentive pay amounts • Favorable total compensation packages relative to those of rival companies • Other nonmonetary productivity-enhancing efforts (see Other Factors)	Annual wages cannot be cut below the required minimums in each geographic region of the world. The minimum annual wage for North America is $18,000; in Europe the minimum is $12,000, and in Asia and Latin America it is $2,500—unless otherwise announced by the game administrator.
Incentive pay per non-defective pair produced	The larger the percentage of total compensation that comes from piecework bonuses, the larger the annual boost to worker productivity. However, once incentive pay exceeds 25% of total compensation, the incremental gains in productivity become progressively smaller and approach 0 as incentive pay approaches 50% of total compensation.	No incentive is paid for defective pairs produced in order to motivate workers to pay close attention to quality and not engage in "hurry-up" procedures that impair footwear quality of the company's products. Higher piecework incentives help reduce the reject rate. The productivity impact of higher or lower incentive pay is indicated in the calculations sections of the production and labor decision screen each time you make an entry for incentive pay.
Total compensation (annual wage plus incentive pay) relative to rivals	Providing higher total compensation relative to competitors has a positive impact on workforce productivity.	Companies with the highest compensation packages (wages plus total incentive pay) are able to attract workers with good experience, skills, and work habits, thus achieving higher levels of productivity than would prevail if the company was on the low end of the industry pay scale.

Other Factors	Impact	Comments
Expenditures to improve production methods	Efforts to improve production methods can lead to productivity gains of as much as 10%, provided ample expenditures are made on an ongoing basis over a period of years. The size of the gain is based on the amount spent on PMI per worker employed at the plant.	It will take sizable expenditures per worker (mainly for training and skills building) over a period of several years to achieve the maximum 10% productivity gain. The productivity gain in any one year is indicated in the calculations sections of the production and labor decisions screen each time you make an entry for PMI.
Hiring additional workers	Raising employment levels at a plant can boost overall plant productivity as much as 2%; however, the bigger the number of new hires, the smaller the gains because the productivity of new workers is lower than that of experienced workers.	Improves morale and job satisfaction; signals better job opportunities and greater job security; boosts company reputation as a "good place to work." However, newly hired workers are lacking in skills and experience compared to existing workers, and a big influx of new hires will dampen net productivity gains.
Laying off workers	Cutting plant employment levels reduces productivity anywhere between 0 and 10%, depending on the percentage of the work force that is laid off. Laying off only a few workers has a minimal effect on productivity—less than 2%.	Layoffs hurt morale and create worker anxiety over job security. Laying off the entire work force and temporarily shutting the plant down will lead to the maximum 10% decline in productivity when the plant resumes operations. The projected impact on productivity associated with layoffs is indicated in the calculations sections of the production and labor decisions screen.

Naturally, increases in the annual wage tend to boost worker productivity. Annual wage increases in the 5-10% range can lead to productivity gains of as much as 6%. However, as the size of the annual wage increase approaches 12% in any one year, the productivity gains flatten out. Past 12%, the only productivity benefit you can gain comes from a more favorable comparison with the compensation packages of rival companies. Wages can be cut to the minimum allowed levels (see the insert on page 45) to try to reduce labor costs but, as you might expect, wage cuts hurt worker productivity—unless offset by other factors. The larger the cut, the bigger the adverse impact because wage cuts boost workforce turnover (some of the company's best workers will leave for better paying jobs elsewhere), reduce the morale and job satisfaction of the remaining work-force, and result in the hiring of less experienced (less productive) workers.

Paying workers a piecework incentive helps reduce reject rates and produces a ***continuing*** boost to worker productivity year after year. A $1.50 per pair bonus incentive offered in Year 11 will motivate workers to produce more pairs in Year 11, and it will motivate them to achieve still higher productivity levels in Year 12, Year 13, and afterward even if the $1.50 incentive is not increased. *Piecework incentives can be used to supplement the minimum annual wage requirements but they cannot be used as a substitute for the payment of the geographic minimums.*

When a company's total compensation package at a particular plant location is below the average of all other footwear companies having plants in the same geographic area, worker morale suffers, the plant will lose some of its best workers to better-paying rivals, and worker productivity at the plant is penalized. The bigger the compensation gap, the greater the adverse effect on productivity at that plant, as the plant's most productive workers leave for better-paying jobs elsewhere. Conversely, when a plant's workers are compensated at annual amounts *above* the geographic region average, worker productivity is greater than it otherwise would be because of the ability to attract and retain higher caliber workers. *The productivity estimates calculated for you on the screen cannot incorporate the impact of whatever changes in compensation that rival companies may make, since there is no way to know what they are going to do. The uncertainty surrounding how your company's compensation package will ultimately compare with that of rival companies is the major reason why the calculated value shown for worker productivity is an estimate rather than a certainty.*

Consequently, you and your co-managers will need to consider carefully the size of annual wage increases, the size of piecework incentives, the percent of total compensation accounted for by incentive pay, and how well your workers are being compensated relative to workers at competing companies (pay comparisons are reported annually in the Footwear Industry Report). However, *judging the effectiveness of compensation decisions by whether they boost or hurt worker productivity misses the mark. The bottom-line objective is to manage the company's compensation program and productivity-enhancing effort to minimize labor costs per pair produced, not maximize the number of pairs each worker produces.* There's little value in undertaking productivity-enhancing efforts that cost more than they are worth. Hence you and your co-managers should always be alert to the effect of compensation decisions and other productivity-related decisions on labor cost per pair produced and on overall manufacturing cost per pair produced.

Decisions to Hire or Lay Off Workers. How many workers are needed at each plant depends on (1) the number of pairs to be produced and (2) the productivity of the workforce (measured by the number of pairs each worker produces on average during a year). Once you and your co-managers have decided on the pairs to be manufactured (which may or may not involve use of overtime) and have made all of the other production and compensation decisions (many of which impact workforce productivity), then you are ready to decide how many workers to employ. Based on the number of pairs you have to be manufactured and the estimated workforce productivity, the maximum number of workers needed is calculated and reported to you on line 4 in the compensation section of the screen (see Exhibit 4-3). The "maximum" number appearing on the screen (line 4) is based on the assumption that paying workers overtime is to be avoided or at least kept to a minimum (in the event that the number of pairs to be produced requires some use of overtime). The "minimum" number of workers shown on line 4 assumes that the overall size of the workforce is to be kept to the lowest possible number and that these workers will work the maximum 20% overtime to produce the desired number of pairs.

Employing fewer workers than the "maximum" needed and relying on some use of overtime acts to reduce plant supervision costs—currently, plant supervision costs per worker employed are $6,000 in North America and $2,000 in the Asian plant. Should you build plants in Europe or Latin America in upcoming years, plant supervision costs will run $5,000 per worker in Europe and $2,000 per worker in Latin America. It is a simple what-ifing exercise to try hiring fewer workers than needed to see if some use of overtime production is economical. Don't be surprised if the answer varies by plant because of the differences in worker compensation and plant supervision costs.

You and your co-managers will have to decide which size workforce between the maximum and minimum values to employ. Increasing total employment in a given year can boost workforce productivity up to 2%, since it signals growing job opportunities and greater job security. Decreasing employment (by laying off workers) has a negative impact on morale and productivity—but the maximum effect even if all workers are laid off and the plant is temporarily shut down is –10%. Note that on 2 lines above the number of workers employed entry in Exhibit 4-3 you are provided the overall productivity estimate for the upcoming year as well as productivity for the prior year. This information gives you a basis for seeing whether the cumulative impact of all your production and labor decisions on productivity, including hiring and layoffs, is positive or negative compared to the prior year.

Actions to Reduce the Reject Rate. The reject rate at each plant is a function of (1) annual quality control expenditures per pair produced, (2) the size of the piecework incentive per pair produced, (3) the number of different models in the company's product line, and (4) a "random" factor that takes into account the somewhat changing mood and morale of the local workforce and whether, on certain given days and weeks, workers are distracted by approaching holidays or adverse weather or internal plant disruptions. The "standard" reject rate is 5.0% at the North American plant and 5.5% at all other plants (unless otherwise announced). But the reject rates at each of your company's plants can differ from "standard" depending on how much you spend on quality control, the piecework incentive, the number of models being produced, and the random factor.

Higher annual quality control expenditures per pair produced tend to reduce the reject rate below the standard, reflecting the benefits of training workers in total quality management techniques. Raising the piecework incentive (say, from $1.00 to $1.25) helps cut reject rates because of increased worker attention to accurate workmanship. Workers are not paid a piecework bonus on pairs which fail final inspection; this policy is a key part of the company's quality control strategy, since it motivates workers to watch the details of what they are doing and not take unwise shortcuts to boost their piecework output. Increasing the number of models produced increases reject rates, owing to more frequent production run changeovers and reduced worker experience in making each model. It is long-standing company policy to donate all defective pairs to charitable organizations; thus, all pairs that fail final inspection represent deadweight cost and lost revenues. As you can see from Exhibit 4-1, in Year 10 there were 168,000 pairs rejected at the company's two plants—equal to a cost of about $213,000 (or about $1.27 per pair as you can see in Exhibit 4-2). The cost impact of rejects is thus significant enough to warrant close management attention.

Temporary Plant Shutdowns. Occasionally market conditions may make it advisable to drastically cut production levels in one or more plants, perhaps even to zero. To *temporarily* shut down production operations at a particular plant, all you have to do is enter a zero for pairs to be manufactured on the manufacturing decisions screen and a zero for the total number of workers employed. Variable costs at the temporarily shut plant will then be zero for the year but your company will still incur full-year depreciation charges and 25% of normal maintenance costs. Company accountants will allocate the fixed costs to corporate overhead (which is, in turn, allocated to all market segments based on pairs sold). When you decide to reopen the plant (it can remain "temporarily shut" for as many years as desired), *worker productivity will resume at about 90% of the worker productivity value that prevailed in the last year of plant operation*.

Plant Upgrades and Capacity Additions

In Exhibit 4-5, a second production-related screen shows involving plant upgrade options, the expansion of existing plants, and the construction of new plants in Europe and Latin America.

Exhibit 4-5

Plant Upgrades / Capacity Additions Screen

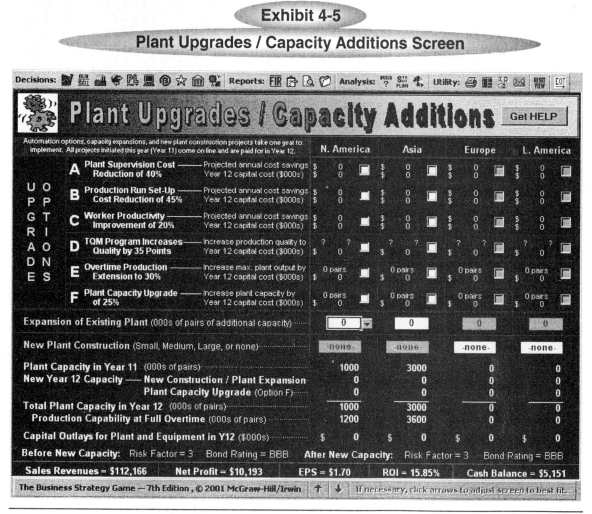

Plant Upgrade Options. There are six options for upgrading existing plants. *Only one option per year may be undertaken at the same plant, and a maximum of three options can be chosen for any one plant.* The nature and cost of the six options are shown in Exhibit 4-6 below. You and your co-managers should take time to assess the merits of each upgrade option because *the cost-saving benefits vary quite significantly from plant to plant and strategy to strategy*.

The costs of plant upgrades are treated as additional investments and have a 20-year service life depreciated on a straight-line basis at the rate of 5% annually. *Upgrade options come on line the year after being ordered.* Payments to the suppliers of upgrade options are made the year the option comes on line (i.e. the year after it is ordered). *An upgrade option can be ordered for a new plant the first year the new plant is on line or any year thereafter; you cannot order upgrades for a new plant in the same year you order its construction.*

Upgrade options are paid for and come on line the year after being ordered.

Exhibit 4-6

Plant Upgrades Options

	Benefits	Capital Investment Requirement and Impact on Annual Depreciation Cost
Option A	Reduces plant supervision costs per worker by 40%	One-time capital investment of $1.75 million per million pairs of plant capacity (has the effect of raising annual depreciation costs by $87,500 per year per million pairs of capacity)
Option B	Reduces production run set-up costs by 45%	One-time capital investment of $3.0 million per million pairs of plant capacity (has the effect of raising annual depreciation costs by $87,500 per year per million pairs of capacity)
Option C	Increases worker productivity by 20%	One-time capital investment of $3.5 million per million pairs of plant capacity (has the effect of raising annual depreciation costs by $175,000 per year per million pairs of capacity)
Option D	Uses new equipment and a TQM program to boost footwear quality by 35 points	One-time capital investment of $4.0 million per million pairs of plant capacity (has the effect of raising annual depreciation costs by $200,000 per year per million pairs of capacity)
Option E	Extends the allowable overtime production percentage from 20% to 30%	One-time capital investment of $2.5 million per million pairs of plant capacity (has the effect of raising annual depreciation costs by $125,000 per year per million pairs of capacity)
Option F	Increases plant capacity by 25%	One-time capital investment of $5.5 million per million pairs of plant capacity (has the effect of raising annual depreciation costs by $275,000 per year per million pairs of capacity)

Plant Construction and Plant Expansion Alternatives. New plants in Europe and Latin America may be constructed in any of three sizes: small (1 million pairs per year), medium (2 million pairs per year), and large (3 million pairs per year). To construct a new plant in Europe or Latin America, simply select Small, Medium, or Large. *Construction of a new plant takes one year.* For example, decision to build a new plant in Year 11 means the plant will come on line ready for full production at the beginning of Year 12. *While your company cannot begin sales and marketing operations in Latin America until Year 12, you can initiate construction of a plant in Latin America in Year 11 in preparation for commencing Latin American operations in Year 12.*

All plants in North America, Asia, Europe, and Latin America, regardless of size, can be expanded in increments of 1 million pairs; *expansions are ready for full production the year after entering the decision to expand.* Hence an expansion ordered in Year 12 is available for full production at the beginning of Year 13. There is no limit on the number of times a plant can be expanded nor is there a limit on the absolute size of a given plant, but *the maximum size of a plant expansion in any one year is 5 million pairs.* Because the North American and Asian plants and any new plants built in Europe or Latin America can be expanded to any size (thereby providing whatever amount of production capacity you desire in any geographic region), *the company is limited to a maximum of four plants*—one in North America, one in Asia, one in Europe, and one in Latin America.

The costs of new plants and plant expansions depend on the year your company initiates construction (as shown in Exhibit 4-7); however, the costs of new plant construction are subject to change (up or down) as the game progresses. The total capital outlays for upgrade options, new plants, and plant expansions are shown in the calculations section of the plant upgrades and construction screen (the light-gray section of Exhibit 4-3). *Payments for new plants and plant expansions are due the year the facilities are available for production (i.e., the year after entering the decision to build or expand).*

Exhibit 4-7

Costs of New Plants and Plant Expansions

	Cost of New Plant Construction			Cost of Plant
	Small (1,000,000 pairs)	**Medium** (2,000,000 pairs)	**Large** (3,000,000 pairs)	**Expansions** (per 1,000,000 pairs)
Year 11	$27,500,000	$54,000,000	$80,000,000	$26,000,000
Year 12	28,500,000	55,900,000	82,800,000	26,900,000
Year 13	29,500,000	57,900,000	85,700,000	27,800,000
Year 14	30,500,000	59,900,000	88,700,000	28,800,000
Year 15	31,600,000	62,000,000	91,800,000	29,800,000
Year 16	32,700,000	64,200,000	95,000,000	30,800,000
Year 17	33,800,000	66,400,000	98,300,000	31,900,000
Year 18	35,000,000	68,700,000	101,700,000	33,000,000
Year 19	36,200,000	71,100,000	105,300,000	34,200,000
Year 20	37,500,000	73,600,000	109,000,000	35,400,000
Year 21	38,800,000	76,200,000	112,800,000	36,600,000
Year 22	40,200,000	78,900,000	116,700,000	37,900,000
Year 23	41,600,000	81,700,000	120,800,000	39,200,000
Year 24	43,100,000	84,600,000	125,000,000	40,600,000
Year 25	44,600,000	87,600,000	129,400,000	42,000,000

These figures reflect price increases of 3.5% annually, rounded to the nearest hundred thousand.

Labor productivity at new European or Latin American plants starts out at 3,000 pairs per worker per year; the reject rate for new plants approximates 5.5% in the first year. In the case of plant expansions, labor productivity and reject rates correspond to those for the existing plant. You and your co-managers are well-advised to analyze whether using overtime to increase production or investing in plant upgrade options E or F is more economical than investing in new plants or plant expansions. For instance, a company with 5 million pairs of capacity that wants to boost production to 6 million pairs may find that unit costs are lower producing at full 20% overtime rather than investing in another 1 million pairs of plant capacity. Likewise, a company with a 3 million-pair plant in Europe may find that utilizing plant upgrade option F to expand capacity by 25% entails lower capital outlays and annual depreciation charges than expanding the plant by another 1 million pairs.

As an aid in helping you analyze the economics of building a new plant or expanding an existing plant, you are strongly encouraged to use the Capacity Construction Analysis option on the Menu Bar—Exhibit 2-3 in Section 2. (We will discuss the use of this option later in Section 8.)

SPECIAL NOTE: Corporate overhead costs rise in stair-step fashion at the rate of $1,000 for each 1,000-pair increase in the company's production capacity (not counting overtime capability). Overhead costs will decline in similar stair-step fashion if capacity additions are subsequently sold or permanently closed.

Buying, Selling, and Closing Plants

You and your co-managers have the option of buying an existing plant from another company, selling all or part of one of your plants to a rival company, or closing a plant and liquidating the equipment. The screen for entering these decisions is shown in Exhibit 4-8.

Exhibit 4-8

Plant Purchase / Sale / Closing Screen

Decisions: Reports: FIR Analysis: Utility:					
BUY $ELL Plant Purchase/Sale/Closing					Get HELP
Purchase of Capacity From Another Company	N. America	Asia	Europe	L. America	Entries for purchase and sale of plant capacity are subject to game administrator approval. If you have an agreement with another company to buy or sell capacity, have the deal approved by the game administrator, who will provide you the password that allows access to the purchase and sale entries.
Company You Are Buying From (company letter)	?	?	?	?	
Capacity Purchased (000s of pairs)	0	0	0	0	
Purchase Price ($000s)	$ 0	$ 0	$ 0	$ 0	
This information provided to you in good faith by selling company. { Avg. Quality Control Expenditure ($ / pair produced)	$ 0.00	$ 0.00	$ 0.00	$ 0.00	
Avg. Methods Imp. Expenditure ($ / pair of capacity)	$ 0.00	$ 0.00	$ 0.00	$ 0.00	
Worker Productivity in Y10 (pairs / worker / year)	0	0	0	0	
Sale of Capacity To Another Company	N. America	Asia	Europe	L. America	
Company You Are Selling To (company letter)	?	?	?	?	
Capacity Sold (000s of pairs)	0	0	0	0	
Selling Price ($000s)	$ 0	$ 0	$ 0	$ 0	
Extraordinary Gain (Loss) on Capacity Sold ($000s)	$ 0	$ 0	$ 0	$ 0	
Permanent Capacity Closing	N. America	Asia	Europe	L. America	Permanently closed capacity is salvaged at 75% of book value (net of depreciation).
Capacity Closed (000s of pairs)	0	0	0	0	
Cash Received for Salvage of Capacity Closed ($000s)	$ 0	$ 0	$ 0	$ 0	
Extraordinary Loss on Capacity Closed ($000s)	$ 0	$ 0	$ 0	$ 0	
All entries on this screen impact Year 11 decision making.	N. America	Asia	Europe	L. America	Overall
Plant Capacity Before Purchase/Sale/Closing (000s of pairs)	1000	3000	0	0	4000
Plant Capacity After Purchase/Sale/Closing (000s of pairs)	1000	3000	0	0	4000
Net Cash Inflows (Outflows) from Purch/Sale/Close ($000s)	$ 0	$ 0	$ 0	$ 0	$ 0
Net Extraordinary Gains (Losses) from Sale/Closing ($000s)	$ 0	$ 0	$ 0	$ 0	$ 0
Sales Revenues = $112,166	**Net Profit = $10,193**	**EPS = $1.70**	**ROI = 15.85%**		**Cash Balance = $5,151**
The Business Strategy Game — 7th Edition, © 2001 McGraw-Hill/Irwin		If necessary, click arrows to adjust screen to best fit.			

Plant Purchases and Sales. Instead of building new plant capacity and paying new-construction prices, you can purchase an entire plant or part of a plant (in multiples of 1 million pairs) from a rival company. Alternatively, you can sell all or part of any plant to a rival company. The price at which existing plant capacity is purchased/sold is a matter of negotiation between the buyer and seller, but the agreed-on price is *subject to approval of your instructor or game administrator* to ensure "arms-length" transactions and prevent "sweetheart deals".

If you negotiate a capacity sale or purchase with a rival company that is approved by your instructor/game administrator, *ownership of the plant will be transferred immediately*; buyers will have immediate use of the capacity and sellers will get immediate use of the proceeds of the sale. *Buying existing plant capacity thus has the distinct advantage of giving you access to additional production capacity quicker than constructing additional capacity.* Plant capacity purchased from another company is treated as having a 20-year life and is depreciated at a 5% annual rate. If the purchaser of plant capacity in a given region already has a plant in that region, the historical quality control, production methods improvements, and worker productivity of the purchased capacity are averaged into the buyer's existing facility. For example, if in Year 14 Company A (which, let us say, operates a 3 million-pair plant in Asia) agrees to purchase Company B's 3 million-pair Asian plant, then in Year 14 Company A will have a 6 million-pair plant in Asia, and worker productivity at the expanded Asia plant will be the weighted average of the productivity levels prevailing at the two plants; the same weighted-average approach also applies to cumulative quality control expenditures per pair and the amounts spent previously for production methods improvement. Also, except for upgrade option C involving worker productivity gains, *all purchased capacity is treated as having no upgrade options* (in other words, the buyer of an existing plant obtains no benefit from upgrade options A, B, D, E, and F that a purchased plant has been equipped with). However, if a buyer already has a plant operating in that same geographic region *and* if the buyer's existing plant has an upgrade option in place, then the upgrade benefits of the buyer's existing plant will automatically be extended to the purchased capacity. Thus, in negotiating for the purchase of an existing plant you will want the buyer to provide you with information about worker productivity, quality control expenditures, and production methods improvement (this data is shown on each company's Manufacturing Report).

> When plant capacity is purchased or sold, the ownership of the capacity and the cash payment are transferred immediately.

All plant capacity purchased must remain in the area where built—you cannot buy all or part of another company's North America plant and move it to Asia; it must remain in North America. To execute a capacity purchase or sale, *first get approval on the price from your instructor or game administrator and obtain the password that will give you access to enter the needed values for plant purchases and sales*.

Any company that sells a plant *below* its undepreciated value (equal to net plant investment as shown on the Manufacturing Report—see Exhibit 4-1) will realize an extraordinary loss; the loss will be reported on the company's income statement in the upcoming year since plant ownership is transferred to the buyer immediately. Since the purchase/sale of plant capacity negotiated and approved in the Year 12 decision period becomes effective in Year 12, it is Year 11's ending net plant investment (or Year 12's beginning plant investment) that is the basis for calculating extraordinary gains and losses. Plant depreciation for Year 12 will be charged to the buyer, not to the seller.

As you can see from looking at the calculations section of Exhibit 4-8, when you finish making entries on the Plant Purchase/Sale/Closing screen, you are provided with a recap of the plant capacity available next year as well as the capital expenditures scheduled at each plant and any extraordinary gains or losses associated with your decisions.

Permanently Closing All or Part of a Plant. In the event you decide it is no longer economical to operate a plant and you are unable to sell it to another company, you have the option to permanently close all or part of a plant (in multiples of 1 million pairs). However, newly obtained capacity must be held on the books for at least one year before it is eligible for *permanent* closing. ***The cash liquidation value of an existing plant is presently 75% of the company's net investment in the facility*** (but this percentage is subject to change as the game progresses—any change will be announced by the instructor/game administrator). The net investment still on the books for each plant is shown on the company's Manufacturing Report. If you wish to permanently close only part of a plant, the investment write-off is prorated by the percentage of plant capacity closed. For example, if you elect to permanently close one-fourth of a 4 million pair plant having a book value of $40,000,000, then the investment write-down will be $10,000,000, the cash liquidation value of the equipment will be $7,500,000, and the extraordinary loss (written off against current earnings) will be $2,500,000

To permanently close a plant, simply indicate how much capacity you wish to shut and at which plant location. Capacity entries are in thousands (enter 1000 to close 1 million pairs of capacity). ***Shutdowns become effective immediately*** (in the same year that the decision is entered), the loss incurred will be charged against current year earnings (appearing as an extraordinary loss on the income statement), and the cash from the liquidation sale will be received and available immediately. Since ***the shutdown occurs at the beginning of the year in which the shutdown decision is made***, the plant capacity in question may not be used for production that year.

Permanent capacity shutdowns take effect at the beginning of the year in which the shutdown decision is entered.

Warehouse and Shipping Operations

All footwear produced at company plants is shipped directly to company-leased warehouses in Memphis, Brussels, and Singapore. Arrangements are being made for a company-leased warehouse to open at the beginning of Year 12 in São Paulo, Brazil, to serve as the distribution center for all Latin American buyers. Each warehouse has sufficient capability to pack and ship whatever order volume can be generated from independent retailers, online buyers, and future retail megastores. Warehouse crews box the shoes, label the boxes, and pack orders for shipment. Buyer orders are shipped on a schedule to meet the company's promised delivery time (1, 2, or 3, or 4 weeks). The pairs available at a particular warehouse can be used only to supply customers in the same geographic area as the warehouse. The more models offered for sale in a geographic region and the shorter the delivery time promised to retailers stocking the company's brand, the more inventory that has to be kept on hand in the warehouse to completely fill orders placed by online buyers and independent retailers for various sizes and styles. Insufficient inventory levels result in longer-than-promised delivery times to independent retailers. A *stockout* occurs whenever the total pairs ordered by area retailers and online buyers exceed the pairs available at the area warehouse (beginning inventory plus incoming shipments from plants). Online buyers and retailers whose orders cannot be filled will immediately place orders in the amount of the stockout with rival companies having pairs available. ***Stockouts reduce the company's service rating in the area the stockout occurs***. The larger the stockout (in percentage terms), the greater the service rating penalty.

Warehouse Operations

Exhibit 5-1 is a copy of your company's Year 10 Warehouse Operations Report. The first section of the report showing beginning and ending inventories and the number of pairs sold is pretty much self-explanatory. The other two sections merit brief discussion.

Exhibit 5-1

The Warehouse Operations Report

	PRIVATE-LABEL	BRANDED WAREHOUSES				OVERALL
		N. A.	Asia	Europe	L. A.	
WAREHOUSE OPERATIONS (000s of pairs)						
Beginning Footwear Inventory	100	23	0	2	0	125
Shipments from ——- North America	0	760	0	0	0	760
Plants　　　　 Asia	400	622	300	550	0	1,872
Europe	0	0	0	0	0	0
Latin America	0	0	0	0	0	0
Pairs Available for Sale	500	1,405	300	552	0	2,757
Pairs Sold ————·Internet (retail)	0	125	24	50	0	199
Wholesale	500	1,125	216	450	0	2,291
Total	500	1,250	240	500	0	2,490
Pairs Liquidated (at the end of Y10)	0	0	0	0	0	0
Ending Footwear Inventory	0	155	60	52	0	267
Warehouse Stockouts	0	0	0	0	0	0
MANUFACTURING COST OF GOODS SOLD ($000s)						
Cost of Beginning Inventory	2,100	552	0	38	0	2,690
+ Cost of Incoming Shipments	8,340	31,105	5,703	10,456	0	55,604
+ Exchange Rate Cost Adjustment	209	306	0	-270	0	245
– Cost of Ending Inventory (before liquidation)	0	3,526	1,141	963	0	5,630
Manufacturing Cost of Goods Sold	10,649	28,437	4,562	9,261	0	52,909
WAREHOUSE EXPENSES ($000s)						
Inventory Storage Charges	25	12	0	1	0	38
Freight on Incoming Pairs	500	1,158	150	688	0	2,496
Import Tariffs	0	0	0	2,200	0	2,200
Warehouse Operations	1,000	3,375	1,480	2,000	0	7,855
Total Warehouse Expenses	1,525	4,545	1,630	4,889	0	12,589
EXCHANGE RATE COST ADJUSTMENTS ($000s)						
Shipments to ——— P-Label —— from Asia	209					209
from Europe	0					0
from L. A.	0					0
N. A. ——— from Asia		306				306
from Europe		0				0
from L. A.		0				0
Asia ——— from N. A.			0			0
from Europe			0			0
from L. A.			0			0
Europe —— from N. A.				0		0
from Asia				-270		-270
from L. A.				0		0
L. A. ——— from N. A.					0	0
from Asia					0	0
from Europe					0	0
Net Impact of Exchange Rate Adjustments	209	306	0	-270	0	245
INVENTORY LIQUIDATION						
$ Per Per Pair ——— Liquidation Price	0.00	0.00	0.00	0.00	0.00	0.00
Liquidated　　 Assigned Cost (see Note 1)	0.00	0.00	0.00	0.00	0.00	0.00
Pre-Tax Profit Impact	0.00	0.00	0.00	0.00	0.00	0.00
Impact ———— Pre-Tax Profit Impact	0	0	0	0	0	0
($000s)　　 Annual Cost Savings (see Note 2)	0	0	0	0	0	0

Note 1: The cost per pair liquidated is the same as the manufacturing cost per pair sold through normal private-label or branded channels. Liquidated pairs are not assigned any warehouse, marketing, administrative, or interest costs.

Note 2: The annual cost savings is an estimate of the storage and finance costs that will be avoided annually.

Manufacturing Costs of Goods Sold. The second section of the Warehouse and Sales Report provides manufacturing cost of goods sold information. As you know, it is standard accounting practice in income statements to base profit-and-loss determination on manufacturing cost of goods *sold* rather than on manufacturing cost of goods *produced*. The two need not be equal. All pairs currently produced may not be sold (some pairs may be left over in inventory), in which case the total dollar value of manufacturing cost of goods produced (as shown in the manufacturing report) can exceed the total dollar value of manufacturing costs of goods sold (as shown in the warehouse and sales report). The reverse occurs when total number of pairs sold in a given year exceeds the number of pairs currently produced and beginning inventories are drawn down to supply the difference between the number sold and the number produced.

Manufacturing costs *per branded pair sold* were higher in the North American market in Year 10 than in Asia or Europe because prior management shipped all non-rejected 760,000 pairs produced at the higher-cost North American plant to the Memphis warehouse for sale as branded footwear in North America. The lower-cost Asian plant supplied all of the footwear sold in Europe, Asia, and the North American private-label market and a substantial fraction of the branded pairs sold in North America. A different pattern of shipment would have resulted in different costs and profit margins in each market. Note also that the cost of ending inventory is subtracted from the cost of pairs available to arrive at the total manufacturing cost of goods sold. The ending inventories in Year 10 are the company's beginning inventories in Year 11 and thus indicate the company's inventory situation as you and your co-managers take charge of the company.

Exchange Rate Adjustments. This item in the manufacturing cost of goods sold section merits careful attention. Exchange rate adjustments result from the company's decision to sell its footwear, produced in one geographic region, in a different geographic region. To handle the necessary foreign currency transactions of global production and marketing operations, the company has established agreements with several global banks to handle its various foreign currency transactions. The agreement covers payments the company receives from buyers in different countries, any currency exchanges arising from constructing and operating plants in various parts of the world, and payments associated with importing or exporting footwear from area to area. The bank agreements call for all of the company's Asian transactions to be tied to the Japanese yen, all European transactions to be tied to the euro, all Latin American transactions to be tied to the Brazilian real, and all North American transactions to be tied to the U.S. dollar.

With help from the company's auditors (a prominent international accounting firm), the company has devised managerial accounting procedures to provide managers with information regarding the impact of exchange rate fluctuations on cross-region shipments. The company's simplified procedure calls for manufacturing costs on footwear shipped between any two geographic regions to be tied to the two corresponding exchanges rates. Thus the manufacturing costs of footwear shipped between North America and Asia are adjusted up or down for exchange rate changes between the U.S. dollar and the Japanese yen; manufacturing costs on pairs shipped between North America and Europe are adjusted up or down based on exchange rate fluctuations between the U.S. dollar and the euro; manufacturing costs on pairs shipped between Asia and Europe are adjusted for fluctuations between the euro and the yen; and so on.

> Fluctuations in exchange rates affect the manufacturing cost of footwear shipped between geographic regions of the world. Exchange rate cost adjustments are calculated and accounted for automatically in the Warehouse Operations Report.

You and your co-managers can track movements in the value of the U.S. dollar against the euro, yen, and real in *The Wall Street Journal* (usually in section C), *USA Today*, and many local newspapers (your instructor/game administrator will inform you about how exchange rate fluctuations will be handled). As you may recall from your earlier studies of exchange rates, when the exchange rate of Japanese yen for U.S. dollars goes down (say from 104.80 yen per dollar to 104.45 yen per dollar), it takes fewer Japanese yen to purchase a U.S. dollar (or, conversely, $1 will exchange for fewer yen). Such an exchange rate change represents a *decline* in the value of the U.S. dollar and *rise* in the value of the Japanese yen. Insofar as your company's footwear business is concerned, a decline in the value of the dollar against the yen makes U.S.-made footwear more competitive in Asia. It takes fewer yen for Asian footwear retailers and consumers to buy U.S.-made shoes when the exchange rate is 100 yen per dollar than when the exchange rate is 105 yen per dollar.

The following statements sum up the effect of fluctuating exchange rates on producing footwear in one geographic region and exporting it for sale in another region:

- A *decline* in the exchange rate of Japanese yen for U.S. dollars enhances the attractiveness of exporting goods from U.S. plants to Asian markets and reduces the attractiveness of producing goods in Asian plants for export to North American markets. Conversely, a *rise* in the exchange rate of yen for dollars reduces the attractiveness of exporting U.S.-made goods to Asia and enhances the attractiveness of exporting Asian-made goods to North America.

- A *decline* in the exchange rate of euros for U.S. dollars enhances the attractiveness of exporting goods from U.S. plants to European markets and reduces the attractiveness of producing goods in European plants for export to North American markets. Conversely, a *rise* in the exchange rate of Eurodollars for U.S. dollars reduces the attractiveness of exporting U.S.-made goods to Europe and enhances the attractiveness of exporting European-made goods to North America.

- A *decline* in the exchange rate of Japanese yen for euros enhances the attractiveness of exporting goods from European plants to Asian markets and reduces the attractiveness of producing goods in Asian plants for export to Europe. Conversely, a *rise* in the exchange rate of yen for euros reduces the attractiveness of exporting European-made goods to Asia and enhances the attractiveness of exporting Asian-made goods to Europe.

- A *decline* in the exchange rate of the Brazilian real for dollars enhances the attractiveness of exporting goods from North American plants to Latin American markets and reduces the attractiveness of producing goods in Latin American plants for export to North America. Conversely, a *rise* in the exchange rate of reals for dollars reduces the attractiveness of exporting North American-made goods to Latin America and enhances the attractiveness of exporting Latin American-made goods to North America.

NOTE: If the exchange rates of Japanese yen for euros or the Brazilian real are not published in the news source you have, you can easily calculate it by dividing the published quote for Japanese yen per U.S. dollar by the quoted exchange rate of euros per U.S. dollar and reals per U.S. dollar. The computer does all the exchange rate calculations for you, however.

As you might expect, the ins and outs of accounting for exchange rate fluctuations in a multinational company become rather complex. To make it easy for you and your co-managers to assess the competitive impact of fluctuating exchange rates on shipping goods produced in one geographic area to distribution centers in another geographic area, company accountants adjust the manufacturing cost of imported footwear upward or downward for the effects of exchange rate fluctuations. Positive numbers for the exchange rate adjustment in the manufacturing cost of goods sold section of the Warehouse and Sales Report reflect an upward cost shift due to competitively adverse exchange rate movements; negative numbers reflect downward cost adjustments and competitively favorable exchange rate shifts.

In effect, the company bears the risk of exchange rate fluctuations. While other currency exchange arrangements could conceivably have been made, an analysis over the years shows that the risk is tolerable. The company's board of directors has decided that the present bank agreements and internal accounting practices concerning foreign exchange transactions will be continued indefinitely.[1] However, you and your co-managers can reduce the company's future exposure to adverse exchange rate fluctuations either (1) by building plants in all of the world's branded markets that you want to serve or (2) by raising/lowering the amounts exported/imported on an annual basis, depending on whether current year exchange rate fluctuations are favorable/unfavorable.

As you can see from Exhibit 5-1, in Year 10 the company had a favorable (negative) exchange rate adjustment of $270,000 on the 550,000 pairs of footwear exported to Europe and an unfavorable (positive) exchange rate adjustment of $306,000 on the 622,000 branded pairs exported from the Asian plant to North America. The –$270,000 figure was derived from the following data:

	Exchange Rate of Euros per Yen	Manufacturing Cost of Pairs Produced in Asia and Shipped to Europe
Year 9	96.320	
Year 10	96.071	$10,456,000

The percentage change in the exchange rate of euros per yen used to calculate the *annual* exchange rate adjustment is adjusted upward by a factor equal to 10 times the actual reported period-to-period percentage change. Multiplying the period-to-period change by a factor of 10 is done as a way of converting the effect of actual exchange rate movements over a period of several days (the interval between your decisions) into a change that represents a full year—the interval over which your company has produced and shipped footwear since the last report. The Year 10 percentage change in the exchange rate of euros per yen, including the factor of 10 adjustment, was calculated thusly:

$$\frac{\text{Year 10} - \text{Year 9}}{\text{Year 9}} \times 10 = \frac{96.071 - 96.320}{96.320} \times 10 = -0.025851 \text{ or } -2.5851\%$$

Applying this percentage change to the $10,456,000 value of Asian-made goods exported to Europe gives:

$$-2.5851\% \times \$10,456,000 = -\$270,302 \quad (\text{or} -\$270,000 \text{ rounded to the nearest thousand})$$

---

[1] *Adjusting manufacturing costs upward/downward in this fashion is a way of approximating the profit impact of fluctuating exchange rates. Strict adherence to financial accounting principles would require adjusting the company's selling prices and revenues instead of costs, but this would have made pricing decisions and price comparisons across companies much harder to interpret. So we opted to use a simplified approach for managerial reporting purposes and avoid the financial accounting intricacies associated with foreign currency transactions. We think you will appreciate the straightforward approach we've taken; it makes decision making easier and approximates closely enough the competitive effects that exchange rate fluctuations have on companies doing business in global markets.*

The positive, cost-increasing exchange rate adjustment of $306,000 on the 622,000 branded pairs exported from the Asian plant to the Memphis warehouse (shown in Exhibit 5-1) is arrived at in similar fashion. An exchange rate change in the yen per dollar from 111.81 in Year 9 to 111.92 in Year 10 works out to be a 0.9838% exchange rate impact, which, when multiplied by shipments of $31,105,000, yields an unfavorable cost-increasing adjustment of $306,000 (rounded to the nearest thousand).[2]

Remember: A positive number for the exchange rate adjustment represents higher costs while a negative number represents lower costs. Consequently, the cost-impacts of exchange rate fluctuations have a bearing on which plants to export from and which regions to export to.

The lesson here is that exchange rate fluctuations have a bearing on costs and profitability. *The bigger the year-to-year changes in the exchange rates between the four currencies, the more that company costs and profitability are affected by how many pairs are exported from which plants to which geographic regions.*

How Exchange Rate Fluctuations Will Affect Future Years. Do not be concerned if the current exchange rates differ greatly from those values pertaining to the Year 10 Warehouse Operations Report. All future exchange rate impacts in the game will be based on actual exchange rate fluctuations in the days and weeks ahead (your instructor will inform you of the starting exchange rate values for Year 11). The Year 10 exchange rates referred to here will thus have no bearing on your company's operating results in Year 11 and beyond. The announced change in the exchange rates from Year 11 to Year 12 will determine exchange rate gains or losses for Year 12; the announced changes from Year 12 to Year 13 will determine the gains or losses in Year 13; and so on. Because the exchange rates announced by your instructor for Year 11 will serve as the base rates for the game, *there will be no exchange rate change impacts on the Year 11 results; the first round of exchange rate gains and losses will come in Year 12*.

Warehouse Expenses. There are four categories of warehouse expenses: inventory storage charges, freight on incoming pairs, import tariffs, and warehouse operating expenses. Each merits brief discussion so you will understand the cost structure underlying your company's warehousing and shipping operations:

- *Inventory storage costs*—Storage charges in any given warehouse are a function of the number of pairs carried over from the previous year; that is, the amount in beginning inventory. Inventory storage costs at *each* warehouse rise in stair-step fashion as the number of unsold pairs carried over to the next year rise. Storage costs are $0.50 per pair for the first 500,000 pairs in unsold inventory carried over from one year to the next; $0.75 for each of the next 250,000 pairs that are carried over; $1.00 per pair on each pair between 750,000 and 1,000,000 pairs; $1.50 on each pair between 1,000,000 and 1,250,000 pairs; and $2.00 on all pairs in excess of 1,250,000 pairs.

- *Freight charges on incoming pairs*—Currently it costs $0.50 per pair to ship footwear from a plant to a warehouse in the *same* geographic area and $1.25 per pair to ship footwear to warehouses in a *different* geographic area.

---

[2]*As you have noted by now, since most of the dollar figures are reported in thousands, rounding to the nearest thousand is standard procedure and accounts for why some of the figures reported are not exact down to the last dollar. Be assured, though, that the rounding "errors" have no material impact on the accounting accuracy of the information presented in the reports. Indeed, we think you will find that having the numbers rounded off to thousands is a welcome simplification.*

- *Tariff costs*—Countries in Europe, Asia, and Latin America currently have imposed tariffs on imported footwear. Tariffs into the European market average $4 per pair; tariffs into Asia currently average $8 per pair; and tariffs into Latin America average $6 per pair. North American governments (the U.S., Canada, and Mexico), believing in the economic benefits of free trade and open markets, do not currently impose tariffs on imported footwear. One reason to locate plants in Europe and Latin America is to escape tariffs on footwear sold in these geographic markets. *All tariffs are paid at the port of entry at the time of shipment even if the goods shipped in remain in the warehouse unsold.* Tariff payments in Year 10 totaled $2,200,000 on shipments to Europe ($4 × 550,000 pairs) and $2,400,000 on shipments to Asia ($8 × 300,000 pairs).

  North American officials have talked to European, Asian, and Latin American governments about the merits of reducing tariff barriers to promote unrestricted free trade, but there is no success to report at this point; discussions will continue. In some parts of the world, there is considerable skepticism about free trade policies; many governments fear that free trade will hurt local industry and increase local unemployment. At this juncture, it is uncertain whether tariff barriers will fall or rise even higher. As the game progresses, *import tariffs in all markets are subject to change.* But it is unlikely that tariffs will change without advance warning. Should any political developments alter the present tariff structure, they will likely be reported in the Footwear Industry Report or announced by your instructor/game administrator.

- *Warehouse operating expenses*—Warehouse operating costs consist of (1) $1 million in annual leasing fees for each distribution center facility (or $5 per pair if the annual volume available for sale in a given region falls below 200,000 branded pairs) and (2) a boxing, packing, and freight charge on each pair shipped to retailers, online buyers, and retail megastores. If a company decides to abandon a given geographic region and no pairs are available for sale in the regional distribution warehouse, the leasing fee is $0; however, if a company later decides to re-enter the region and resume sales, the 20-year leasing agreement provides for adequate warehousing space to be made available immediately at the customary fee of $ million annually or $5 per pair, whichever is smaller. There's an added $500,000 leasing fee for the private-label section of the Memphis warehouse (or $5 per pair if the annual volume made available for sale falls below 100,000 pairs); the leasing fee for private-label warehousing and shipping space drops to $0 if a company withdraws from the private-label segment and has no private-label pairs available in this section of the Memphis warehouse. Company accountants have analyzed warehouse activities and found that there are scale economies in each warehouse's order-filling process. Labor, materials and equipment, and outbound freight costs average $2 per pair on the first million pairs, $1.50 per pair on the next 2 million pairs, and $1 per pair on all shipments from the same warehouse in excess of 3 million pairs annually.

Shipping Decisions

The central issue you and your co-managers must wrestle with on the shipping decisions screen in Exhibit 5-2 is where to ship all the pairs produced to (1) be able to supply the forecasted demand in each market segment and satisfy the related inventory requirements, (2) make sure each warehouse is stocked with the optimum number of models and footwear quality, and (3) optimize the impact of exchange rate fluctuations on costs and profitability. All branded footwear produced must be shipped to one of the company's distribution warehouses; footwear cannot be shipped in a later year from one warehouse to another. ***All private-label pairs produced are automatically routed to the Memphis warehouse in North America—no decision entries on your part are needed.*** As always, below the decision entries on the Shipping Decisions screen is a series of calculations (updated with each entry) showing the projected outcomes associated with your decision entries.

> **Once finished goods have been shipped to a warehouse, they must be sold from that warehouse; footwear cannot be re-shipped in a later year from one warehouse to another.**

Exhibit 5-2

Shipping and Warehouse Screen

Decisions: ... Reports: ... Analysis: ... Utility: ...

Shipping & Warehouse   Get HELP

All private-label pairs are automatically shipped to the Private-Label Warehouse. You need only specify branded shipments from plants to branded warehouses. The number of pairs awaiting shipment from each plant is shown below in parentheses.

	P-Label Warehouse	Branded Warehouses			
		N. America	Asia	Europe	L. America
Forecasted Demand for Year 11 (see Demand Forecast screen)	650	1409	451	564	0
Plus Inventory Required to Achieve Desired Delivery Time	0	99	25	39	0
Less Beginning Footwear Inventories (carried over from Y10)	0	155	60	52	0
Minimum Footwear Shipment (given demand and inventory needs)	650	1353	416	551	0
Branded Pairs Available — N. American Plant ( ) to	0	760	0	0	0
to Ship From Plants Asian Plant (12) to	399	622	300	550	0
(000s of pairs) European Plant (0) to	0	0	0	0	0
L. American Plant (0) to	0	0	0	0	0
Total Pairs Shipped (should be ≥ minimum footwear shipment figure)	399	1382	300	550	0
Beginning Inventory (5 point or 10 point quality penalty applied)	0	155	60	52	0
Pairs Available for Sale (beginning inventory + incoming shipments)	399	1539	362	606	0
Quality Rating of Pairs Available for Sale (weighted average)	78	94	90	90	0
Model Availability of Pairs Available for Sale (weighted average)	100	100	100	100	0
Warehouse Costs — Inventory Storage Cost	$ 0	$ 78	$ 30	$ 26	$ 0
(000s of $) Freight on Incoming Shipments	499	1162	151	693	0
Import Tariffs	0	0	0	2216	0
Warehouse Operations Expenses	899	3614	1724	2128	0
Total Warehouse Costs	$ 1398	$ 4854	$ 1905	$ 5063	$ 0
Total Warehouse Cost Per Pair Available for Sale	$ 3.50	$ 3.15	$ 5.26	$ 8.35	$ 0.00
Exchange Rate Cost Impact Per Pair Available for Sale	$ 0.00	$ 0.00	$ 0.00	$ 0.00	$ 0.00

Sales Revenues = $112,166	Net Profit = $10,193	EPS = $1.70	ROI = 15.85%	Cash Balance = $5,151

The Business Strategy Game — 7th Edition , © 2001 McGraw-Hill/Irwin   ↑   ↓   If necessary, click arrows to adjust screen to best fit.

Going into Year 11, you have no pairs of private-label shoes in inventory, 155,000 pairs of branded shoes in inventory in North America, 60,000 branded pairs in Asia, and 52,000 branded pairs in Europe. ***The warehouse in Latin America will not be operational until Year 12, so no shipments to Latin America can be made in Year 11.*** Keep in mind that unless each distribution warehouse has sufficient inventory to fill all incoming orders, your company will experience stockouts. Stockouts have three adverse consequences: (1) your company loses sales that it could have gotten otherwise, (2) buyers whose orders are unfilled will immediately try to obtain the wanted number of pairs from competitors with inventories available (i.e., rival companies will pick up the sales you lost), and (3) your company's service rating will be penalized. To help you avoid stockouts and to meet the inventory requirements to achieve desired delivery times, there's information just above the shipping decision entries to keep you informed as to the number of branded pairs needed in each warehouse and the minimum number of pairs that should be shipped to each distribution location.

Furthermore, as you enter the pairs to be shipped from the company's plants to the company's distribution warehouses, the calculations section on the shipping decision will immediately provide you with the weighted average quality ratings and model availabilities of all pairs (including leftover inventories) available for sale in the warehouse serving each customer/market segment. This allows you to adjust shipments until you end up with the desired quality ratings and model availabilities in each warehouse. There is a wealth of information in the calculations section of the shipping decisions screen to guide your choices of how much to ship where so as to optimize the resulting quality, number of models, inventory levels, costs, and exchange rate impacts.

The Importance of Good Inventory Management. Cutting inventories too thin runs the risk of stockouts (if your demand forecast proves too low). Furthermore, there are minimum inventory requirements to achieve 1-week, 2-week, and 3-week delivery times to retailers (one of the factors in the service rating); failure to maintain the required inventory minimums results in failure to achieve the desired delivery times and a lower service rating. Shipping just the minimum pairs runs the further risk that the reject rate will turn out higher than expected (the reject rate projections on the production and labor decisions screens are accurate only within ±0.5%), causing a shortfall in the pairs available for shipment and inability to ship all the pairs you requested. If the actual number of non-defective pairs produced turns out to be different from the expected number of non-defective pairs, then the quantities shipped to each warehouse will automatically be increased or decreased *proportionally* to bring total shipments into equality with total pairs available for shipment.

At the other extreme, allowing unsold inventories to mushroom out of control is costly in two respects. One, inventory storage costs rise as unsold inventory rises. Two, there is a 5-point quality rating penalty applied to unsold private-label pairs and a 10-point penalty is applied to unsold branded pairs—these penalties are to reflect the fact that unsold pairs are last-year's models and styles, making them less attractive to buyers. (The quality rating penalties are factored into the quality ratings reported on the Shipping Decisions screen.)

You and your co-managers are thus well advised to exercise prudent inventory management practices.

Sales and Marketing Operations

You and your co-managers can market the company's products through any or all of four distribution channels:

- North American chain stores that purchase athletic footwear for sale under their own private-label.

- Independent footwear retailers who carry athletic footwear for sale to consumers, such as department stores, retail shoe stores, sporting goods stores, and pro shops at golf and tennis clubs.

- Online sales at the company's Web site.

- Company-owned and operated retail "megastores."

This section describes the company's sales and marketing operations and explains the decision-making options you will have each year. *Keep in mind that your company cannot begin sales and marketing operations in Latin America until Year 12.*

Private-Label Marketing Decisions

Currently, private-label retailers require a quality rating of at least 50 and model availability of 50 of all bidders (these specifications are subject to change as the game progresses). The maximum bid price that chain store buyers will accept is $2.50 below the average wholesale price that companies charge independent retail dealers for branded footwear in North America; without a significant price break on their wholesale purchases of private-label footwear, chain stores can make more profit selling branded footwear.

Bids from companies whose private-label warehouse stock does not meet buyer specs (currently a quality rating of 50 or greater and a model availability of 50 or greater) are automatically rejected. Also, bid prices must be at least $2.50 below the average branded *wholesale* price in North America.

If you and your co-managers elect to enter bids to supply private-label footwear to chain discounters, there are two decisions to be made annually: (1) how many pairs to offer to chain stores and (2) what price to bid. The private-label decision entries are shown in Exhibit 6-1. Bids from companies which meet all buyer specifications are starting with the lowest-priced bidder and then accepting each ascending bid until either total chain store demand for private-label footwear is satisfied or all qualified bids are accepted, whichever occurs first. If you decide to bid for the private-label business of chain stores, (1) enter a bid price down to the penny and (2) indicate the quantity your company is willing to offer at that price (always in thousands of pairs). Depending on the amount chain stores are buying, the price bids of rivals, and the various quantities offered, your company may sell all of the pairs offered to private-label buyers, some of the pairs offered, or nothing. In the case of tie bids on price, chain store buyers will opt for the supplier whose products have the highest quality rating; if there are ties on both price and quality, the award goes to the supplier offering the highest number of models. *Unsold private-label pairs remain in inventory and you can try to sell them in the following year's bidding process. Storage costs for unsold pairs and the standard 5-point quality rating reduction for unsold pairs will apply.*

If two or more companies bid the same price, the tie goes to the bidder with the highest private-label quality rating; if both price and quality are the same, model availability serves as the second tie-breaker.

The Option to Liquidate Private-Label Inventories. In the event that your company is unsuccessful in selling portions of your private-label inventory, there is an option to liquidate surplus pairs at distressed-merchandise prices. To see the current-year terms of the liquidation option at any time, simply click on the liquidation option button on the screen. A dialog box will appear explaining the option and showing the liquidation price that inventory liquidators are willing to pay for your excess pairs—the liquidation price varies from year to year according to a variety of conditions. The dialog box will also provide you with an estimate of the potential savings on storage costs and inventory financing. The liquidation price will typically be *below* the cost incurred to manufacture the pairs and will not cover any shipping, import tariff, marketing, administrative, or interest costs that might be associated with the inventory to be liquidated. Therefore, you and your co-managers will probably find it advantageous to try to sell the private-label inventory through regular channels before resorting to liquidation. If the liquidation terms are acceptable, simply leave the liquidation button in the "on" position. To reject the liquidation option, click the button to the "off" position.

Exhibit 6-1
Private-Label Marketing Decisions Screen

Decisions: [icons] Reports: [icons] Analysis: [icons] Utility: [icons]

Private-Label Marketing [Get HELP]

IMPORTANT NOTE: Bids from companies whose private-label warehouse stock do not meet these minimim buyer specs are automatically thrown out.

Private-Label Buyer —— Quality Rating 50
Specifications Model Availability 50

Private-Label Warehouse Analysis	Pairs (000s)	Quality Rating	Model Availability
Beginning Inventory (carried over from Year 10 and includes 5 point quality rating penalty)	0	0	0
Incoming Footwear Shipments (manufactured and shipped in Year 11)	399	78	100
Pairs Available for Sale (quality and model figures are weighted averages)	399	78	100

Bid for Private-Label Market —— Pairs Offered for Sale (000s) — 500
Bid Price ($ per pair offered) — $ 34.00

REMEMBER: If you go back and change production decisions, double-check this screen to be sure your weighted average quality and models remain above the minimum specs.

Projected Pairs Sold (the smaller of pairs available, pairs offered, or your demand forecast) — 399
Projected Ending Inventory (subject to a 5 point quality penalty if carried over to Year 12) — 0

Inventory Liquidation Option (click the button to toggle on/off and view option details) — **Option Off**

Revenue-Cost-Profit Analysis (000s of $)		Revenue-Cost-Profit Analysis ($ per pair sold)	
Revenues	$ 13566	Revenues	$ 34.00
Manufacturing Cost	8740	Manufacturing Cost	21.90
Warehouse Cost	1398	Warehouse Cost	3.50
Administrative Cost	748	Administrative Cost	1.87
Total Operating Cost	10886	Total Operating Cost	27.28
Operating Profit	2680	Operating Profit	6.72
Interest Expense (Income)	837	Interest Expense	2.10
Income Taxes	553	Income Taxes	1.39
Net Profit	$ 1290	Net Profit	$ 3.23

| Sales Revenues = $112,166 | Net Profit = $10,193 | EPS = $1.70 | ROI = 15.85% | Cash Balance = $5,151 |

The Business Strategy Game — 7th Edition , © 2001 McGraw-Hill/Irwin ↑ ↓ If necessary, click arrows to adjust screen to best fit.

Internet Marketing Decisions

The company's recent effort to begin selling its footwear has been an encouraging success to this point. In Year 10, the company sold nearly 200,000 pairs online at a price of $60.00 and realized per pair profits of $7.50 on shipments to online buyers in North America, $5.42 on sales to European buyers, and $5.78 on sales to buyers in Asia. On an industry-wide basis, the *total online sales (all companies combined) could rise to as much as 11% of branded sales in each geographic region in Year 11 and to as much as 12% of global branded sales in Year 12.* You'll be provided a 5-year demand forecast at the end of Year 11 showing each year's potential online sales percentage (for reasons of simplicity, this percentage will apply equally to all four geographic regions of the world market). Bear in mind that the total number of pairs that all companies are likely to sell online will top out at 20% of total branded demand in any one year.

The Internet Marketing Decision screen is shown in Exhibit 6-2. Management must make three decisions each year regarding the company's online sales effort:

- What average retail price to charge for the models and styles available for purchase at the company's Web site.

③ Year 11 internet sales to 11% of branded & 12% in year 12

→ Max at 20% in any one year

- How many models and styles to offer for purchase.
- How fast to deliver the online orders placed by customers.

You'll find the assortment of onscreen calculations and information valuable in arriving at an attractive online sales strategy.

Exhibit 6-2

Internet Marketing Screen

Decisions: | Reports: FIR | Analysis: BUILD ? STR PLAN | Utility: | RESET VIEW | EXIT

Internet Marketing

Get HELP

Direct marketing through company web site: www.?.com

	N. Amer.	Asia	Europe	L. Amer.
Ratings and Features of Branded Pairs ─── Image Rating	46	65	45	0
Available for Sale Quality Rating	94	90	90	0
Model Availability	100	100	100	0

	Year 11	Year 10
Internet Marketing ─── Internet Price ($ per pair)	$ 60.00	$ 60.00
Effort Models Offered (50 to 100)	75	75
Delivery Option (A, B, C, or D)	C	C

	N. Amer.	Asia	Europe	L. Amer.
Warehouse Operations ── Branded Pairs Available for Sale	1539	362	606	0
in Year 11 (000s) Projected Internet Sales (direct to retail customers)	156	42	62	0
Pairs Available for Sale to Branded Retailers	1383	320	544	0

	N. Amer.	Asia	Europe	L. Amer.
Revenue-Cost-Profit ── Revenues	$ 9360	$ 2520	$ 3720	$ 0
Projections Manufacturing COGS	3672	833	1231	0
($000s) Warehouse Expenses	537	221	557	0
Marketing and Expenses	2713	729	1100	0
Administrative Expenses	292	79	116	0
Interest and Taxes	772	250	278	0
Net Profit	$ 1373	$ 408	$ 439	$ 0

ACCOUNTING NOTE: Manufacturing costs, warehouse expenses, marketing expenses, administrative expenses, and interest expenses are allocated to each internet region based on its percentage of total pairs sold. Income taxes are allocated to each internet region based on regional contribution to pre-tax profit.

	N. Amer.	Asia	Europe	L. Amer.
Revenue-Cost-Profit ── Revenues	$ 60.00	$ 60.00	$ 60.00	$ 0.00
Projections Manufacturing COGS	23.54	19.83	19.85	0.00
($ / pair sold) Warehouse Expenses	3.45	5.27	8.98	0.00
Marketing and Expenses	17.39	17.36	17.74	0.00
Administrative Expenses	1.87	1.87	1.87	0.00
Interest and Taxes	4.95	5.96	4.48	0.00
Net Profit	$ 8.80	$ 9.71	$ 7.07	$ 0.00

Sales Revenues = $112,166	Net Profit = $10,193	EPS = $1.70	ROI = 15.85%	Cash Balance = $5,151

The Business Strategy Game — 7th Edition , © 2001 McGraw-Hill/Irwin ↑ ↓ If necessary, click arrows to adjust screen to best fit.

The share of total online sales in each geographic region that your company is able to capture is a function of three global factors and three region-specific factors. The three global determinants of the unit volume sold online are (1) how the number of different models and styles offered at your company's Web site compares against the breadth of models and styles offered at competing Web sites, (2) the company's average retail sales price for these models and styles as compared to the average retail prices of models offered at the Web sites of rival companies, and (3) how well the speed of delivery promised by your company (next-day air, 3-day air/ground, 1-week standard, and 2-week economy shipping) stack up with the speed of delivery promised by rival companies. The three region-specific factors are how your company's product quality, image rating, and advertising in the buyer's region of the world market compares with those of rival sellers. Shipments to online buyers are always made from the distribution warehouse serving the buyer's geographic region. Since the average quality of footwear in each regional warehouse can vary from region to region, as can the company's image rating and advertising, it is logical that these three region-specific factors come into play in determining online sales in each part of the world market for branded footwear.

First, you and your co-managers must decide the average price for models offered for sale on the company's Web site. In effect, the price you enter represents an average *retail* price of all the models that are available for sale online. *How your online price compares with the online prices of competing companies is the single most important determinant of your company's share of the online sales segment.* Studies show that a big percentage of online buyers are bargain-hunters and are quite sensitive to price differences—it is very easy for them to click over to the Web sites of rivals and check out how your prices compare. *The maximum allowed price for models and styles sold at the company's Web site is $150 per pair.*

A second decision you and your co-managers must make concerns how many models to offer for sale at the company's Web site. The *maximum* number of models you can offer for sale to online buyers equals the minimum number of models available in the warehouses in the regions in which you are currently marketing branded footwear and have inventory available for sale. This number is tracked by the computer and reported on the screen just to the left of the decision entry cell. The minimum number of models in any one warehouse becomes the maximum number of models marketed online because shipments to online buyers are always made from the distribution warehouse serving the buyer's geographic region and because the company, for cost reasons, has only a single worldwide Web site rather than a Web site for each geographic region. However, you can choose to offer fewer than the maximum number of models to online buyers to economize on the costs of Web site operations—offering fewer models online means having fewer pictures and product descriptions, fewer pages to design and create, and so forth. You can check the on-screen calculations to see the cost-savings associated with offering fewer models and thus determine what number of models to include in your online offering. If you want to increase the number of models offered online beyond the maximum number shown on the screen, you can go back to the production and shipping screens and produce more models and/or adjust your shipping pattern to increase the minimum number of models available at the warehouse that is setting the maximum limit on the online number of models offered.

The third online marketing decision concerns the delivery time you promise to online buyers. The cost of 2-week economy shipping is $7 per pair for each pair sold and shipped to online buyers. The $7 charge represents the cost of picking the order from the proper storage bin in the distribution warehouse, packaging the order for shipping, labeling, and making the necessary arrangements with transportation providers. Faster delivery entails added costs: 1-week "standard" delivery increases order fulfillment and shipping costs of $10 per pair; the total order processing and shipping cost for 3-day air/ground delivery is $13 per pair, and next-day air costs $16 per pair.

The more favorably that your company's product quality, image rating, and advertising in a given region compare with those of rival footwear companies and the more favorably that your company's average online retail sales price, models offered, and delivery times compare with those of competitors, the bigger your online sales volume and online market share will be. In the unlikely event that you and your co-managers wish to abandon selling in the online segment of the footwear market, then simply enter a zero for the average selling price—this entry will be interpreted by the computer as your decision to not offer any branded pairs for sale at the company's Web site.

Branded Marketing Decisions

Decisions regarding branded marketing have a far-reaching impact on the strength of your company's competitive effort relative to rivals and the attractiveness of your company's branded footwear as compared to competing brands. The Year 10 decisions of prior management are shown on the branded marketing decisions screen in Exhibit 6-3. Below the boxed decision entries on the branded marketing screen is an assortment of calculations (updated with each entry) showing the projected outcomes associated with your decision entries.

Exhibit 6-3

Branded Marketing Decisions Screen

Decisions: Reports: FIR Analysis: BUILD? STR PLAN Utility: RESET VIEW EXIT

Ⓑ Branded Marketing   Get HELP

	North America		Asia		Europe		Latin America	
	Year 11	Year 10	Year 11	Year 10	Year 11	Year 10	Year 11	Year 10
Ratings and Features of Branded — Image Rating	46	50	65	50	45	50	0	0
Pairs Available for Sale Quality Rating	94	100	90	100	90	100	0	0
Model Availability	100	100	100	100	100	100	0	0
M Wholesale Price to Retailers ($ per pair)	$40.00	$40.00	$40.00	$40.00	$40.00	$40.00	$0.00	$0.00
A Promo — Advertising Budget (000s of $)	$2000	$2000	$500	$500	$1000	$1000	$0	$0
R Rebate Offer ($0 to $10 per pair)	$3	$3	$1	$1	$2	$2	$0	$0
K Point of — Number of Retail Outlets	5000	5000	500	500	1000	1000	0	0
E Sale New Company-Owned Stores (20 max)	0	0	0	0	0	0	0	0
T Total Company-Owned Stores	0	0	0	0	0	0	0	0
I Service — Dealer Support and Online Services	$500	$500	$50	$50	$100	$100	$0	$0
N Desired Delivery Time (4, 3, 2, 1 week)	3 weeks	3 weeks	3 weeks	3 weeks	3 weeks	3 weeks	0 weeks	0 weeks
G Projected Delivery Time (Y10 is actual)	3 weeks	3 weeks	4 weeks	3 weeks	3 weeks	3 weeks	0 weeks	0 weeks
Projected Service Rating (Y10 is actual)	94	100	94	100	94	100	0	0
Branded Pairs Available for Sale (after iNet sales)	1383	Delivery Time	320	Delivery Time	544	Delivery Time	0	Delivery Time
Wholesale Projected Pairs Sold (branded wholesale)	1253	Requirement	320	Requirement	502	Requirement	0	Requirement
(000s of pairs) Projected Ending Inventory (or stockout)	130	99			42	39	0	0
Inventory Liquidation Option (click to toggle on/off)	Option is Off		Option is Off		Option is Off		Option is Off	
Projected Regional — Revenues	$ 50120	$40.00	$ 12800	$40.00	$ 20080	$40.00	$ 0	$ 0.00
Revenue-Cost-Profit Manufacturing COGS	29492	23.54	6343	19.82	9968	19.86	0	0.00
The numbers in the first column rep- Warehouse Expenses	4317	3.44	1684	5.26	4506	8.98	0	0.00
resent total dollars (in thousands) Marketing Expenses	6534	5.21	581	1.82	1592	3.17	0	0.00
and the numbers in the second col- Administrative Expenses	2348	1.87	599	1.87	941	1.87	0	0.00
umn represent dollars per pair sold. Interest and Taxes	4169	3.33	1556	4.86	1687	3.36	0	0.00
Net Profit	$ 3261	$ 2.60	$ 2036	$ 6.36	$ 1386	$ 2.76	$ 0	$ 0.00

| Sales Revenues = $112,166 | Net Profit = $10,193 | EPS = $1.70 | ROI = 15.85% | Cash Balance = $5,151 |

The Business Strategy Game — 7th Edition , © 2001 McGraw-Hill/Irwin ↑ ↓ If necessary, click arrows to adjust screen to best fit.

Pricing Decisions. Since it would be unwieldy to set separate prices for each of the models and styles of athletic footwear your company produces, you and your co-mangers will need to set only an "average" or "blended" wholesale/retail price for the entire product line in a particular geographic region. While prior management tended to sell its footwear at the same average wholesale price in North America, Asia, and Europe, *you have the discretion to charge different prices in different geographic regions* should you wish, for any reason, to do so. The single average price that you set for a geographic region will apply both for sales to independent dealers and for branded footwear sales at company-owned retail megastores (should you elect to pursue this distribution channel).

You should think of the revenue per pair that the company derives from sales to independent retailers as being strictly a wholesale price; retailers typically mark up the shoes by 100% over the wholesale price they pay you to arrive at their retail list price. Thus, if your average wholesale price to independent retailers is $40 per pair, the retail list prices of your various models and styles will typically average $80 per pair. The advantage of selling through company-owned retail megastores is that the net revenue per pair to the company is the retail price at the megastore. Thus, should you and your co-managers elect to open retail megastores in a particular geographic region, the price entered on the decision screen will, in effect, become an average wholesale/retail selling price for the company's entire product line offering in a particular geographic area—in other words, it will represent a blend of the wholesale price to retail dealers and the retail price at company-owned retail megastores. As will be explained in greater detail below when we describe the retail megastore marketing option, having a sizable company-owned chain of retail megastores gives you the ability to set a higher wholesale/retail price than if you decide to sell exclusively through independent retail dealers and realize only a wholesale price on each branded pair shipped to retailers.

The maximum average price you can charge per branded pair is $99.99. This maximum applies to all four geographic regions. There is no limit on how much you can raise or lower price from one year to the next. If you do not want to sell any pairs in a particular geographic area, simply enter a zero price for that area and cut back your marketing efforts to zero (or to whatever amounts you wish to spend anyway).

Keep in mind the importance of pricing your branded footwear at levels that will be competitive with the footwear offerings of rival companies. *Your company's average wholesale price relative to competitors is the single most important determinant of sales volume and market share.* The more your company's wholesale price in a geographic region is above the region average, the more shoppers who otherwise are attracted to your brand will be drawn to lower-priced brands with comparable attributes. Nonetheless, a higher-than-average price can be partially or wholly offset by a combination of higher quality, better service to independent retailers, extra advertising, bigger customer rebates, a better brand image, the addition of more models to your company's product line, a more aggressive online sales effort, and a larger network of retail outlets and retail megastores. But the further your company's prices are above the industry average, the harder it is to overcome buyer resistance to a higher price and avoid a loss in market share.

Advertising Decisions. Your company can gain a competitive advantage over rivals in capturing market share by outspending them on advertising and thereby making your company's brand better known and more widely recognized. Advertising strengthens brand awareness, helps steer shoe buyers to retail stores carrying your company's brand, and informs people about the company's latest styles and models. The competitive impact of advertising depends on the size of your company's current-year advertising budget. The company's market aggressiveness in promoting its lineup of models and styles in a given geographic area will be judged stronger when annual advertising expenditures *exceed* the area average and is judged weaker the further its ad budget is *below* what rival companies are spending on average. Of course, you have to be careful that greater advertising expenditures don't get costs out of line or reduce overall profitability—there are diminishing marginal benefits from outspending rivals on advertising by a wider and wider margin. Enter all advertising expenditures in thousands of dollars (for example, enter 2500 to spend $2,500,000 on advertising). Keep in mind that cumulative advertising over all years carries a 60% weighting in the International Footwear Federation's calculations of company image ratings.

Decisions Regarding Customer Rebates. Offering rebates to the consumers who purchase your company's shoes is a way to differentiate your product offering from rivals and potentially create competitive advantage. If you elect to employ promotional rebates,

Rebate Offer	Redemption Rate	Cost Per Pair Sold
$ 1	15%	$0.15
2	20	0.40
3	25	0.75
4	30	1.20
5	35	1.75
6	40	2.40
7	45	3.15
8	50	4.00
9	55	4.95
10	60	6.00

you have ten options ranging from as little as $1 to as much as $10 per pair. All rebate offers must be in round dollars. Deciding against use of a rebate is always an option. Different rebates can be used in each geographic market. Customer response to rebates is a function of (1) the size of the rebate (rebates in the $8 to $10 range will generate a more than proportional market share response compared to $3 to $5 rebates) and (2) the amount by which your company's rebate is above/below the average rebate in that geographic market. *Since all buyers will not mail in the rebate coupon, the per pair cost of a promotional rebate is below the face value of the coupon (see the table to the right).*

Decisions Regarding Retail Outlets. The more independent retail outlets a company has carrying its brand of shoes, the more exposure your brand has to consumers and the easier it is for them to find a nearby store from which to purchase your company's footwear. Currently, your company has 5,000 North American retail outlets, 500 Asian outlets, and 1,000 European outlets. The upper limit on the number of retail outlets you can have in an area is 99,999 (which should prove more than ample). While having more retail outlets is generally better than having fewer outlets, there are diminishing marginal benefits to having progressively more retail outlets than rivals. Having a below-average number of retail dealers is not necessarily fatal to gaining a decent market share; a company can generate substantial sales in a geographic area with as few as 100 retail outlets (assumed to be located in large metropolitan areas), provided the company's shoe line is otherwise amply attractive to consumers and provided it has an attractive Web site offering for online sales and perhaps also utilizes retail megastores to supplement its network of independent shoe retailers.

The entries for retail outlets represent the total number *(these entries are not made in thousands)*. If you decide you want 6,000 North American dealers, then enter 6000 (not 6). At present, retailer support costs equal $100 for each retail outlet the company has in North America, Asia, Europe, and Latin America but this cost is subject to change as the game progresses. The dealer support cost represents the costs of providing retailers with in-store promotional materials, creating catalogs, furnishing store clerks with sales information, and maintaining current credit ratings for each retailer. *All other competitive factors being equal, companies with larger numbers of retail outlets in a given geographic region will outsell companies with smaller retail networks.*

Decisions Regarding Company-Owned Retail Megastores. You and your co-managers have the option of opening company-owned retail megastores to supplement the branded sales effort of independent retailers and to build branded sales and market share. There's credible marketing research indicating that opening two-level 14,000 square-foot company-operated stores in high-traffic, upscale shopping centers and shopping malls in North America, Europe, Asia, and Latin America will materially enhance the company's brand name visibility in local retail markets and have a strongly positive effect on unit sales volume. As explained in Section 2, the format for these stores entails a festive, energetic in-store shopping environment, a miniature running track, and a half-court basketball area to promote high volumes of customer traffic and grow unit sales volume. One important sales-increasing advantage of such stores is that they give your company an effective way to showcase its entire lineup of models and styles (most independent footwear retailers stock only selected models and styles in your company's product line-up). A second big advantage is that a chain of company-owned megastores allows you and your co-managers to set a somewhat higher average wholesale/retail selling price (to account for the fact that the company sells its footwear at retail in company-owned stores). *Other competitive factors being equal (price, quality, advertising, and so on), the latest marketing research indicates that companies with more retail megastores will outsell companies with fewer such stores and will be able to charge a higher average wholesale/retail price.*

You and your co-managers can use the demand-forecasting model to arrive at reasonable estimates of the sales-increasing effect of building a chain of company-owned megastores in a particular geographic region. Bear in mind that there is no hard and firm number of pairs of branded shoes that can be sold with a particular number of company-owned megastores because this varies according your company's overall competitive effort (average selling price, quality, models, advertising, number of retail dealers, and so on) and according to the combined competitive effort of rival companies (how many megastores they have, the size of their retail dealer network, their prices, their product quality, and so on).

Should you and your co-managers elect to open retail megastores in a particular geographic region, the price entered on the decision screen will, in effect, become an average wholesale/retail selling price for the company's entire product line offering in a particular geographic area. In other words, it represents a blend of the wholesale price to retail dealers and the retail price at company-owned retail megastores. The more megastores you have in a region, other things being equal, the higher the average wholesale/retail price you can charge without depressing unit sales. The latest and best available marketing research indicates that a chain of *approximately 100 company megastores will be needed in a particular geographic region to be able to charge a blended wholesale/retail price of $5 above what could be charged by relying exclusively on independent retailers* and realizing only an average wholesale price on each branded pair shipped to retailers.

However, marketing research further indicates that there are no more than 1,000 attractive retail locations for megastores in each of the four geographic regions and that these locations are not all equally attractive. Once the combined total of all company-owned stores in a region passes 500, there will be diminishing marginal gains to adding more megastores. If rival footwear companies should open a combined total of more than 1,000 retail megastores in any one geographic market, there will be no discernible gain in overall sales and market share owing to store saturation effects. Moreover, the more retail megastores that you have in any one geographic region, the more that buyers of your company's brand will divide their purchases both among retail dealers and company-owned retail megastores. In others words, the two types of retail distribution outlets compete with each other for the patronage of footwear buyers. So, a strategy of adding large number of retail dealers and also opening a sizable number of retail megastores is likely to result in diminishing marginal benefits from the standpoint of increasing overall sales volume. Independent retail dealers take a dim view of company efforts to build a chain of retail megastores in their geographic region because they see such stores diluting their own sales; as a consequence, the more retail megastores your company has in a particular geographic region, the less that independent retailers will push your company's brands in their stores and the weaker their overall sales-increasing effect will be. You can go to the demand forecasting screen and do some "what-ifing" to arrive at estimates of the sales trade-off between company-owned megastores and retail dealers and to try to arrive at an optimum combination of retailers and company-owned stores.

You and your co-managers will find that opening and operating a chain of company-owned stores entails a commitment of significant financial resources. The up-front investment costs and ongoing operating expenses of company-owned stores are as follows:

- Capital investment of $500,000 per company-owned retail store for furnishings, fixtures, and cash register systems (the $500,000 per store capital cost applies to all four geographic regions of the world market). This investment is depreciated at the rate of 5% annually.

- Annual leasing fees of $120,000 for company-owned stores in North America and Europe and $60,000 for stores in Asia and Latin America.

- Annual maintenance costs of $25,000 per store (5% of gross capital investment).

- Annual wages and salaries for North American and European store personnel starting at $500,000 per store in Year 11 and escalating at 2.5% each year thereafter to account for wage increases and inflation.

- Annual wages and salaries for store personnel in Asia and Latin America starting at $250,000 per store in Year 11 and, likewise, escalating at 2.5% each year.

At present, any one company is **limited to opening no more than 20 retail megastores per year in any one geographic area (or a total of 80 such stores per year worldwide)**. This limitation may be adjusted up or down by your instructor/game administrator in the years to follow. However, given the costs of opening and operating such stores, you are unlikely to find this limitation very confining. Later on, should you decide to alter your sales and marketing strategy for branded footwear, you have the option of closing some or all of the company-owned retail stores previously opened. By closing down stores, the company can immediately escape payment of leasing fees, store maintenance costs, and the payment of annual wages and salaries, but the company's undepreciated capital investment in stores that are closed will have **a liquidation or salvage value of only 10% of the investment** still remaining on the books. The write-off of 90% of the undepreciated investment in closed stores will be charged against earnings in the year the stores are closed. Since the losses could prove sizable if you open and then subsequently close a large number of company-owned megastores, there's merit in being prudent and cautious in opening new stores unless and until you and your co-managers are confident that the financial investment in company-owned stores will prove profitable.

The calculations provided on the Branded Marketing Decision screen and trial-and-error "what-ifing" on the Demand Forecasting screen will help you and your co-managers assess the economics of opening company-owned megastores and in evaluating the trade-offs between utilizing retail dealers and utilizing company megastores.

Decisions Regarding Retailer Support and Online Service. If one element of your company's competitive strategy is to boost your company's service rating above the present levels of 100 in North America, Asia, and Europe and thereby gain more promotional support from retailers in merchandising your footwear, then one strategy-implementing action you and your co-managers can take is to devote greater resources to retailer support and online services. Such expenditures go for staffing the customer service department, providing representatives with up-to-date communications technology, and seeing that they have the online information and problem-solving skills needed to please and delight the company's retail dealers and retail megastore personnel. The company's retailer support and online service representatives are available online or via telephone and fax to handle inquiries, take orders, oversee the order fulfillment process, and resolve any problems that arise with dealers.

Year 10 expenditures for retailer support and online service totaled $500,000 in North America, $50,000 in Asia, and $100,000 in Europe—amounts equal to the International Footwear Federation's standard of $500 per dealer in each geographic region. The caliber of service effort your company makes to provide retailers with satisfactory service is one of the three factors used by the International Footwear Federation in calculating the company's service rating. (You may wish to refer back to Exhibit 3-1 on page 30 for more details on how the service rating is calculated.)

While in prior years the company's expenditures of $500 per retail dealer resulted in adequate service and few dealer complaints, this effort level has not produced any competitive edge for the company and it has not dampened dealer grumbling about the "channel conflict" posed by the company's recent online sales effort. Many independent retailers are convinced the recent growth of online sales at the company's Web site and mounting traffic at the Web site from visitors browsing the company's product offering are cutting into their own sales growth and profit opportunities.

Expenditures for dealer support and online services above the federation's benchmark of $500 per retail dealer will boost your service rating, and expenditures below the $500 standard will penalize your service rating. Just as you would expect, there are diminishing marginal increases in the service rating from progressively larger expenditures for dealer support and online services. As you make your decision entries for dealer support and online services, the on-screen calculations will provide you with the estimated effect these expenditure levels will have on the company's service rating in each geographic region.

Decisions Regarding Delivery Time. Retailers consider a delivery time of 4 weeks as "satisfactory." The costs of 4-week delivery are built into the per-pair costs of warehouse operations. Shorter delivery times will boost your company's service rating, but entail added costs. Currently, *3-week delivery entails an added cost of $0.50 per pair, 2-week delivery costs $1.25 per pair, and 1-week delivery costs $2.00 per pair*; these costs are subject to change as the game progresses. However, *the more models in your product line and the shorter the delivery time you try to achieve, the bigger the inventory your company must have in each distribution center to be able to completely fill retailer orders for various sizes and styles*. The onscreen calculations keep you apprised of the inventory required to achieve the desired delivery times to retail dealers. If your estimated ending inventory levels are below the required levels, you will have to decide whether to lengthen the desired delivery time, to increase production and build up warehouse inventories to the needed levels, or live with the prospects of a lower service rating for next year. Remember that inventory storage costs rise progressively as unsold finished goods inventory rises—per pair inventory storage costs *at each warehouse* are $0.50 per pair for the first 500,000 pairs in unsold inventory, $0.75 for the next 250,000 pairs, $1.00 on every pair between 750,000 and 1,000,000, $1.50 on every pair between 1,000,000 and 1,250,000, and $1.50 on each unsold pair in excess of 1,250,000 pairs.

The Inventory Liquidation Option. In the event that your company is unsuccessful in selling portions of your branded footwear inventory, there is an option to liquidate unwanted inventory at any distribution warehouse at below-market prices. When you click on the liquidation option button on the screen, a dialog box will appear explaining the option and showing the price that inventory liquidators are willing to pay for surplus footwear. Just as with private label inventory liquidation, the liquidation price for branded footwear surpluses at a particular distribution warehouse varies from year to year according to a variety of conditions. The dialog box will also provide you with an estimate of the potential savings on storage costs and inventory financing. Since the liquidation price will typically be *below* the cost incurred to manufacture the pairs and will not cover any shipping, import tariff, marketing, administrative, or interest costs that might be associated with the inventory to be liquidated, you and your co-managers will find it advantageous to try to sell the branded pairs in the open market and use liquidation only as a desperate last resort. If you want to pursue liquidation and find the liquidation terms acceptable, simply leave the liquidation button in the "on" position. To reject the option, click the button to the "off" position.

Bids For Celebrities

Twelve new celebrity sports figures from all over the world have indicated their willingness to wear a company's athletic footwear and endorse its brand in company ads if the fee they are paid is sufficiently attractive. All of the available sports personalities have hired agents to represent them in a competitive bidding process to decide whose brand they will endorse. The screen shown in Exhibit 6-4 provides the information needed to participate in the bid process if you and your co-managers are interested. Contract bids for three well-known sports celebrities will take place in Year 11; the remaining nine celebrities will be bid for in upcoming years according to the schedule shown in the next to last column of Exhibit 6-4.

While all of the 12 celebrities are known worldwide, the extent to which consumers recognize them and are influenced by whose products they endorse varies according to the *consumer appeal index* shown on the screen—the endorsement influence of each celebrity has the same market impact in each geographic region (for reasons of simplicity). A celebrity with a consumer appeal index of 100 will have twice as much market impact as one with an index of 50. Signing several high-profile celebrities has a strong positive impact on your company's brand image rating—celebrity endorsements carry a 40% weight in the International Footwear Federation's image rating calculation. The higher the sum of the consumer appeal indexes of the celebrity endorsers your company signs, the higher your company's overall brand image rating and the greater the branded sales volume that can be achieved (other things being equal). There is no limit on the number of celebrities that can be signed by a particular company. However, there is a rapidly diminishing market impact associated with signing additional celebrities once the sum of their consumer appeal indexes rises above 400. Whether the incremental sales and profits contributed by a celebrity endorser are sufficient to cover the contract fees paid will, of course, depend on how high you have to bid to win the celebrity's endorsement. There is credible market research indicating that the value of celebrity endorsements in the athletic footwear business will have a positive bottom-line payoff if the contract fees that win endorsements are not unreasonably high.

If your are the winning bidder for the services of a particular celebrity, the celebrity will be available in the year following your winning bid and you will begin to pay the celebrity's annual contract cost in the year following your winning bid—no costs other than the bid fee are incurred in the year of the bid.

The standard contract periods vary by celebrity as you can see from the decision screen in Exhibit 6-4. All contract offers are based on the dollars to be paid to the celebrity each year of the contract; celebrities will sign with the company making the highest offer (subject to a required minimum of $500,000 per year). In the event of ties in the highest offer, the celebrity will sign with the company whose celebrity endorsers have the *lowest* combined consumer appeal indexes (if the high bidders have celebrity endorsers with the same combined consumer appeal indexes, the celebrity will sign with the company having the *lowest* overall image rating). The preference of celebrity endorsers to sign with companies having a weaker lineup of endorsers reflects their belief that this will give them greater overall exposure as the company's principal spokesperson. The potential for ties argues for odd-number contract offers. Your company will incur a cost of $100,000 for each bid it submits for a celebrity's services; this cost is subject to change as the game progresses.

Exhibit 6-4
Celebrity Endorsement Bid Screen

Celebrity	Consumer Appeal Index	Standard Contract Length	Company Currently Holding Contract	Year Signed	Terms ($000s/year)	Year Next Available For Bids	Contract Offer ($000s/year)
Payton Manyon	60	2 years	[unsigned]	---	$ 0	Year 11	$ 0
Oprah Letterman	100	3 years	[unsigned]	---	0	Year 11	$ 0
Mia Jamm	70	5 years	[unsigned]	---	0	Year 11	$ 0
Tiger Green	90	2 years	[unsigned]	---	0	Year 12	$ 0
José Montana	50	3 years	[unsigned]	---	0	Year 12	$ 0
Karioki Footsu	100	4 years	[unsigned]	---	0	Year 12	$ 0
Freon Deon	40	1 year	[unsigned]	---	0	Year 13	$ 0
Venus Volley	55	3 years	[unsigned]	---	0	Year 13	$ 0
Cheryl Hoops	75	4 years	[unsigned]	---	0	Year 13	$ 0
Jaques LaFeet	30	2 years	[unsigned]	---	0	Year 13	$ 0
Pélé Payless	60	3 years	[unsigned]	---	0	Year 14	$ 0
Mikee Nikee	80	4 years	[unsigned]	---	0	Year 14	$ 0

Recent Celebrity Bidding History	Celebrity	Year Last Bid For	No. of Bidders	High Bid	2nd Bid	Avg. Bid	Low Bid
	Payton Manyon	---	0	0	0	0	0
	Oprah Letterman	---	0	0	0	0	0
	Mia Jamm	---	0	0	0	0	0
	Tiger Green	---	0	0	0	0	0
	José Montana	---	0	0	0	0	0
	Karioki Footsu	---	0	0	0	0	0
	Freon Deon	---	0	0	0	0	0
	Venus Volley	---	0	0	0	0	0
	Cheryl Hoops	---	0	0	0	0	0
	Jaques LaFeet	---	0	0	0	0	0
	Pélé Payless	---	0	0	0	0	0
	Mikee Nikee	---	0	0	0	0	0

The minimum acceptable contract offer for any one celebrity is $500 thousand. The cost to prepare each contract offer is $100 thousand, payable the year the offer is made.

Year 11 Celebrity Endorsement Costs

Existing Contracts	$ 0
Bidding Preparation Cost	0
Total Endorsement Cost	$ 0
Per Branded Pair Sold	$ 0.00

Potential Year 12 Endorsement Costs

New + Existing Contracts	$ 0
Per Branded Pair Sold	$ 0.00

Sales Revenues = $112,166	Net Profit = $10,193	EPS = $1.70	ROI = 15.85%	Cash Balance = $5,151

The Business Strategy Game — 7th Edition, © 2001 McGraw-Hill/Irwin   ↑ ↓   If necessary, click arrows to adjust screen to best fit.

Reports Concerning Marketing Operations

After each year's decisions, you and your co-managers will be provided with three marketing-related reports: the Marketing and Administrative Report, the Cost Analysis Report, and the Geographic Profit Analysis report. You'll find the information in all three reports valuable in tracking the effectiveness of your marketing strategy and in improving the cost effectiveness of the company's sales and marketing operations.

The Marketing and Administrative Report. Exhibit 6-5 shows the Year 10 Marketing and Administrative Report. The first section reports the expenses associated with operating the company's Web site and fulfilling orders placed at the Web site. There are several things you need to know about the cost structure of Web site operations:

- Server/domain lease fees—The company leases state-of-the-art servers to handle site traffic and also has arrangements with Web hosting providers for shopping cart software, credit card processing, and Web site security. These fees vary according to the amount of traffic at the company's Web site and the number of pairs actually ordered. Lease fees can be expected to run about $1 million annually, given your company's present sales volume and share of the online market. Higher volumes and a higher share of the online market produce somewhat higher fees, and lower sales volumes result in lower fees. Company-wide costs for server/domain lease fees are allocated to each of the geographic regions based on each region's respective percentage of total pairs sold online.

- Web site maintenance and support—Company accountants have determined that the costs for Web site maintenance and support average $8,000 per model offered for sale. The costs cover providing pictures and multilingual descriptions of each model, giving site users a choice of languages in which to view the site, and keeping the site design refreshed every 3 or 4 months and convenient to use. In Year 10, the company offered 75 models for sale producing costs of $600,000 for Web site maintenance and support. These costs are allocated to each of the geographic regions based on their respective percentage of total pairs sold online.

- Order processing and delivery—Order fulfillment costs are $7 per pair sold when the company employs economy two-week delivery. Faster delivery entails added costs. Order processing and delivery costs are $10 for "standard" 1-week delivery, $13 for 3-day air/ground delivery, and $16 for next-day air delivery. (Prior management employed standard 1-week delivery in Year 10; this produced costs of $1,990,000 for the 199,000 pairs sold online.)

The second section of the report provides data for keeping track of the number of company-owned retail megastores in each geographic region, the company's investment in megastores and annual operating costs associated with whatever megastores you and your co-managers have elected to open.

The third section of the report provides a marketing expense summary. Most of the expense numbers are straightforward but the calculations underlying several merit brief explanation. The customer rebate redemption costs in Year 10 resulted from prior management's decision to institute rebate incentives of $3 in North America, $2 in Europe, and $1 in Asia. In North America, 25% of shoe buyers redeemed the $3 rebate coupons, creating redemption costs of $938,000 ($3 × 25% participation rate × 1,250,000 pairs sold).[1] The $36,000 in redemption costs in Asia represented a 15% return of the $1 rebate on 240,000 pairs sold. In Europe 20% of the $2 rebates on the 500,000 pairs sold were redeemed, resulting in redemption costs of $200,000. The Year 10 costs for retailer support and online services were based on $100 in retailer support services for each outlet handling the company's brands plus discretionary expenditures for retailer support—see Exhibit 6-3.

Costs for on-time delivery arise out of managerial decisions to accelerate delivery of customer orders for branded shoes from the 4-week standard (the costs of which are included in the order-filling charge) to 3 weeks, 2 weeks, or 1 week. Prior management

---

[1]*Since all customers do not bother to redeem rebates, redemption costs are less than the face value of the coupons multiplied by the number of pairs sold. The rebate redemption percentages are listed on page 69 of this manual.*

opted for 3-week delivery, resulting in added delivery costs of $0.50 per pair on the 1,125,000 branded shipped to independent retailers in North America, the 216,000 pairs sold and shipped to Asian retailers, and the 450,000 pairs delivered to European retailers.

Exhibit 6-5

Marketing and Administrative Report

	N. A.	ASIA	EUROPE	L. A.	OVERALL
INTERNET MARKETING EXPENSES ($000s)					
Server / Domain Lease Fees	565	154	231	0	950
Web Site Maintenance and Support	357	97	146	0	600
Order Processing and Delivery	1,250	240	500	0	1,990
Total Internet Marketing Expenses	2,172	491	877	0	3,540
COMPANY-OWNED MALL MEGASTORES					
Number of ——— At the End of Year 9	0	0	0	0	0
Stores New Stores Added in Year 10	0	0	0	0	0
Total Stores for Year 10	0	0	0	0	0
Property and —— Year 9 Net Investment	0	0	0	0	0
Fixtures Investment in New Stores	0	0	0	0	0
($000s) Depreciation in Year 10	0	0	0	0	0
Year 10 Net Investment	0	0	0	0	0
Operating ———·Wages and Salaries	0	0	0	0	0
Expenses Operations (lease, utilities, maintenance)	0	0	0	0	0
($000s) Depreciation (of property and fixtures)	0	0	0	0	0
Total Operating Expenses	0	0	0	0	0
MARKETING EXPENSES ($000s)					
Internet Marketing Expenses	2,172	491	877	0	3,540
Company-Owned Store Operations	0	0	0	0	0
Advertising Expenditures	2,000	500	1,000	0	3,500
Customer Rebate Redemption	1,013	43	225	0	1,281
Retailer Support and Online Services	3,000	75	200	0	3,275
On-Time Delivery Expenses	563	108	225	0	896
Celebrity Endorsement Expenses	0	0	0	0	0
Total Marketing Expenses	8,748	1,217	2,527	0	12,492
ADMINISTRATIVE EXPENSES ($000s)					
Executive Salaries					900
Other Corporate Overhead					3,000
Total Administrative Expenses					3,900

The company has two categories of administrative expenses: executive salaries and corporate overhead (not including interest expenses). Executive salaries totaled $900,000 in Year 10; in future years executive salaries will be equal to 1% of companywide revenues or $900,000, whichever is larger. Corporate overhead represents the costs incurred for accounting, information technology, headquarters office space and supplies, travel and entertainment, legal fees, and assorted other administrative costs. Corporate overhead, currently $3 million per year, increases in stair-step fashion at the rate of $1 million for each 1 million pairs of added production capacity (not including overtime), and also will include the fixed costs of any temporarily closed plants. Overhead will be reduced proportionately when capacity is sold or permanently shut down.

The Cost Analysis Report. The Cost Analysis Report provides you and your co-managers with a detailed breakdown of the costs per pair sold in the private-label market and in each geographic market. The lower portion of the Cost Analysis Report for Year 10 is shown in Exhibit 6-6.

Exhibit 6-6

The Cost Analysis Report

	PRIVATE LABEL	N. AMERICA iNet	N. AMERICA Whsle.	ASIA iNet	ASIA Whsle.	EUROPE iNet	EUROPE Whsle.	L. AMERICA iNet	L. AMERICA Whsle.	OVERALL
Production (weighted by shipments)	20.85	22.51	22.51	19.01	19.01	19.01	19.01	0.00	0.00	21.12
Exchange Rate Adjustment	0.52	0.22	0.22	0.00	0.00	-0.49	-0.49	0.00	0.00	0.09
Inv. Cost Adjustment (Note 1)	-0.07	0.02	0.02	0.00	0.00	0.00	0.00	0.00	0.00	0.02
Mfg. Cost Per Pair Sold	21.30	22.75	22.75	19.01	19.01	18.52	18.52	0.00	0.00	21.23
Whse. — **Inventory Storage**	0.05	0.01	0.01	0.00	0.00	0.00	0.00	0.00	0.00	0.02
Costs Shipping (average)	1.00	0.93	0.93	0.63	0.63	1.38	1.38	0.00	0.00	1.00
Tariffs (average)	0.00	0.00	0.00	0.00	0.00	4.40	4.40	0.00	0.00	0.88
Operations	2.00	2.70	2.70	6.17	6.17	4.00	4.00	0.00	0.00	3.15
Total	3.05	3.64	3.64	6.79	6.79	9.78	9.78	0.00	0.00	5.06
Mkt. — — **Internet Marketing**	0.00	17.38	0.00	20.46	0.00	17.54	0.00	0.00	0.00	1.42
Costs Mall Mega-Stores	0.00	0.00	0.00	0.00	0.00	0.00	0.00	0.00	0.00	0.00
Advertising	0.00	1.60	1.60	2.08	2.08	2.00	2.00	0.00	0.00	1.41
Rebates	0.00	0.00	0.90	0.00	0.20	0.00	0.50	0.00	0.00	0.51
Retailer Suport	0.00	0.00	2.67	0.00	0.35	0.00	0.44	0.00	0.00	1.32
On-Time Delivery	0.00	0.00	0.50	0.00	0.50	0.00	0.50	0.00	0.00	0.36
Celebrity Endor.	0.00	0.00	0.00	0.00	0.00	0.00	0.00	0.00	0.00	0.00
Total	0.00	18.98	5.67	22.54	3.13	19.54	3.44	0.00	0.00	5.02
Administrative Expenses	1.57	1.57	1.57	1.57	1.57	1.57	1.57	0.00	0.00	1.57
Interest Expense (Income)	2.34	2.34	2.34	2.34	2.34	2.34	2.34	0.00	0.00	2.34
Total Cost Per Pair Sold	28.26	49.27	35.96	52.25	32.84	51.75	35.65	0.00	0.00	35.21

There are several aspects of the Cost Analysis report that merit your attention:

- The production costs per pair of $20.85 for private-label shoes and $19.01 for branded shoes in Europe and Asia were below the $22.51 branded cost in North America in Year 10 because all shipments to Europe and Asia and to the private-label segment were from the company's lower-cost Asian plant. As discussed in Section 4, exchange rate adjustments in Year 10 unfavorably impacted the company's costs of shipments from Asia to North America and favorably impacted the costs of shipments to Europe. The sum of current production costs per pair, the exchange rate adjustment, and the inventory cost adjustment equals the unit manufacturing costs of goods sold. In Year 10, manufacturing costs per branded pair sold differed significantly across the three geographic markets— from a low of $18.52 in Europe to a high of $22.75 in the North American branded segment.

- *It is standard accounting practice at your company to charge all operating costs incurred in a given year to the pairs sold in that year.* Even though shipping charges are $0.50 per pair on pairs shipped within geographic regions and $1.25 per pair on shipments across geographic regions, the shipping costs *per pair sold* may turn out to be more or less than $0.50 or $1.25 because (1) the pairs sold in a region may represent a blend of pairs produced at a plant within the same region and in other regions and (2) the number of pairs shipped to a given warehouse in a given year is not the same as the number of pairs sold in that same region. In Year 10, shipping costs per pair of $1.38 exceeded the $1.25 cost to ship each pair because standard accounting practice calls for charging the entire cost of shipping the 550,000 pairs into Europe from Asia to the 500,000 of those pairs that were sold. This accounting practice causes the per pair shipping cost to be higher than $1.25 in Year 10, but because the shipping cost of the unsold 50,000 pairs in the European warehouse have already been charged to Year 10 operating costs, the company's shipping cost in Europe in Year 11 will be lower than they otherwise would have been.

Even though the tariffs on pairs shipped are $4 into Europe, $8 into Asia (and $6 into Latin America), the cost of tariffs per pair sold can be higher or lower than the actual tariff because tariffs in any given year are paid when the pairs are shipped not when the pairs are sold. For example, in Year 10 tariffs on European sales averaged $4.40 per pair sold (instead of $4.00) because the company paid tariffs of $4 per pair on the 550,000 pairs shipped from Asia to Europe (thus incurring costs of $2,200,000) but the company only sold 500,000 pairs in Europe in Year 10. The full $2,200,000 in tariff costs incurred on Year 10 shipments to Europe were thus charged to the 500,000 pairs sold in Europe in Year 10, producing unit costs of $4.40 per pair rather than $4.00.

- *All marketing costs in North America are allocated to branded sales because no such expenses are needed to win private-label sales.*

- The costs of advertising are allocated both to online sales and to branded sales made through regular retail channels (independent dealers and company-owned megastores) based on the percentage of total branded pairs sold through each type of distribution channel. Hence, if the breakdown of branded pairs sold in a particular geographic region was 8% online and 92% through traditional brick-and-mortar retailers, the 8% of advertising costs would be allocated to the region's online segment and 92% would be allocated to sales made through regular channels. Online sales are allocated a portion of advertising because the company's image rating (which is a function of cumulative advertising) is one of the factors affecting online sales.

- Likewise, should your company employ celebrities to endorse and promote the company's brand in upcoming years, then the costs of celebrity endorsements will be allocated to each geographic region in which branded pairs are sold based on the percentage of total branded pairs sold in each geographic region. The influence of celebrity endorsements has a 40% weighting in determining the company's image rating. Further, the costs of celebrity endorsements within each geographic region will be allocated partly to online sales and partly to sales through brick-and-mortar retail channels based on the percentage of branded pairs sold online and the percentage sold through independent retailers and company-owned megastores.

- The sales and marketing costs incurred for company-owned megastores, rebate redemptions, retailer support, and on-time delivery to independent footwear retailers are assigned totally to branded sales through brick-and-mortar channels.

- Administrative expenses and interest costs are allocated to private-label sales, online sales in each geographic region, and to branded sales through brick-and-mortar channels based on the percentage of total pairs sold in each different market segment. Allocating administrative and interest costs to each segment based on each segment's share of pairs sold has the effect of making unit costs for these cost items the same in each segment.

The Geographic Profit Analysis Report. The purpose of the Geographic Profit Analysis Report is to keep you informed about the company's revenue, overall unit costs, and profits (or losses) per pair sold in each of the nine different segments of the world footwear market. As you can see from the Year 10 report in Exhibit 6-7, it provides you with a convenient, easy-to-understand breakdown of the company's sales revenue per pair sold, per pair operating costs by category (manufacturing, distribution, marketing, and administrative), and operating profits and net profit per pair for private-label sales and for branded sales (both online and through traditional brick-and-mortar retailers) in each region of the world market. Much of the data for the Geographic Profit Analysis Report comes from information contained in the Cost Analysis Report.

Exhibit 6-7

The Geographic Profit Analysis Report

REVENUE-COST-PROFIT ANALYSIS ($ per pair sold)	PRIVATE LABEL	N. AMERICA		ASIA		EUROPE		L. AMERICA		OVERALL
		iNet	Whsle.	iNet	Whsle.	iNet	Whsle.	iNet	Whsle.	
Sales Revenues	34.00	60.00	40.00	60.00	40.00	60.00	40.00	0.00	0.00	40.39
Oper. ——· Manufacturing	21.30	22.75	22.75	19.01	19.01	18.52	18.52	0.00	0.00	21.25
Costs Distribution	3.05	3.64	3.64	6.79	6.79	9.78	9.78	0.00	0.00	5.06
Marketing	0.00	18.98	5.67	22.54	3.13	19.54	3.44	0.00	0.00	5.02
Administrative	1.57	1.57	1.57	1.57	1.57	1.57	1.57	0.00	0.00	1.57
Operating Profit	8.09	13.07	6.38	10.09	9.50	10.59	6.69	0.00	0.00	7.51
Extraordinary Gain (Loss)	0.00	0.00	0.00	0.00	0.00	0.00	0.00	0.00	0.00	0.00
Interest Income (Expense)	-2.34	-2.34	-2.34	-2.34	-2.34	-2.34	-2.34	0.00	0.00	-2.34
Pre-Tax Profit	5.74	10.73	4.04	7.75	7.16	8.25	4.35	0.00	0.00	5.16
Income Taxes	1.72	3.22	1.21	2.32	2.15	2.48	1.30	0.00	0.00	1.55
Net Profit	4.02	7.51	2.83	5.42	5.01	5.78	3.04	0.00	0.00	3.61

In Year 10 the company earned the greatest wholesale profit per pair (a margin of $5.01) by selling branded pairs to Asian retailers—this was principally because all of the branded pairs sold in Asia were produced at the company's Asian plant where manufacturing costs per branded pair were significantly lower as compare to those made at the North American plant. The most profitable internet segment was the in North America where profits averaged $7.51 per pair sold. The least profitable segment was the $2.83 per pair profit earned on wholesale sales to North American retailers. Note that Europe had significantly higher distribution costs ($9.78 versus $6.79 for Asia and $3.64 for North America); the $6 tariff on all pairs shipped to Europe was the primary cause of the higher distribution costs.

Financing Company Operations

Once you and your co-managers have made all the needed operating decisions for plant operations, warehouse operations, and sales and marketing operations, you are ready to go to the Finance and Cash Flow Decision screen. There you will initiate whatever financing activities you deem appropriate to support your operating and capital investment decisions. Going into Year 11, the company's finances were in good order. In Year 10, the company earned $1.50 per share and paid an annual dividend of $0.40 per share. The company's common stock price has been trading around $15 per share. The company has a very respectable BBB bond rating.

Don't be surprised if internal cash flows from time to time prove inadequate to cover all the capital improvements that you and your co-executives want to undertake. The company has the financial strength to raise new capital by issuing additional long-term debt (bonds), by issuing new shares of common stock, or by taking out a short-term loan. As an alternative, you could decide to freeze or reduce the annual dividend to generate more funds internally for funding expansion and capital improvements. If interest rates are sufficiently favorable, you'll want to consider refinancing some of the company's outstanding bonds at lower interest rates. If new capital requirements are modest and the company has ample financial strength, you and your co-managers may wish to boost EPS by repurchasing some of the outstanding shares of common stock or to make early payments on some of the company's bonds to reduce annual interest costs.

How you and your co-managers handle the financing of company operations has a big impact on the company's bond rating, the interest rates your company pays on new bond issues and short-term loans, the company's return on investment, and the company's stock price. Before you rush into these decisions, familiarize yourself with the company's most recent financial statements.

The Income Statement

Exhibit 7-1 presents the company's Income Statement for Year 10. There are several things worth noting:

- Revenues for the year totaled $100,580,000, operating profit was $18,690,000, and net income after taxes was $9,000,000. North American branded footwear sales contributed 47.1% of total operating profits ($8,812,000 out of $18,690,000), making it far and away the company's most important market segment.

- ***The company pays an income tax rate of 30%.*** Taxes owed are calculated as a straight 30% of income before taxes. After-tax losses may be carried over for ***three*** years in determining your company's tax liability. Thus, if your company should have an after-tax loss of $500,000 in one year, your company will have a $500,000 tax-loss carry-forward to deduct against before-tax income the following three years until the $500,000 "tax credit" is used up.

Exhibit 7-1

The Income Statement

Thousands of Dollars	PRIVATE-LABEL	BRANDED N. A.	Asia	Europe	L. A.	OVERALL
Revenues from Footwear Sales	17,000	52,500	10,080	21,000	0	100,580
Manufacturing Cost of Goods Sold	10,649	28,437	4,562	9,261	0	52,909
Warehouse Expenses	1,525	4,545	1,630	4,889	0	12,589
Marketing Expenses	0	8,748	1,217	2,527	0	12,492
Administrative Expenses	783	1,958	376	783	0	3,900
Operating Profit (Loss)	4,043	8,812	2,295	3,540	0	18,690
Extraordinary Gain (Loss)						0
Interest Income (Expense)						-5,833
Income Before Taxes						12,857
Income Taxes						3,857
Net Income						9,000
Earnings Per Share (\$ per share)						1.50

- An extraordinary gain (loss) arises when your company permanently closes a plant or company-owned megastores or when you sell plant capacity above or below the prevailing book value for that capacity. Gains or losses on plant sales and investment write-offs on the closing of plants and/or company megastores are accounted for as an extraordinary item and affect before-tax income. For instance, if you and your co-managers negotiate the sale of all or part of a plant at a price ***above*** the company's remaining net investment in the plant, then your company realizes a taxable extraordinary gain on the transaction equal to the difference between selling price and net investment on the books. (The net investment in each plant appears on each year's Manufacturing Report.) If you and your co-managers sell plant capacity to another company at a price *below* its net investment value, then your company incurs a loss equal to the difference between the sales price and the remaining net investment on the books. When a plant is permanently closed, the liquidation value is 75% of net investment; the liquidation value of retail megastore furnishings and fixtures is 10% of the remaining net investment. The write-offs associated with a plant shutdown or store closings appear on the Income Statement as an extraordinary loss in the year the facilities are closed.

The Cash Flow Report

The Cash Flow Report provides a convenient summary of annual cash inflows and annual cash disbursements—see Exhibit 7-2 for the company's Year 10 Cash Flow Report. Total cash available from all sources amounted to $100,077,000 in Year 10. Total cash outflows in Year 10 were $100,044,000, leaving the company with a small cash balance of $33,000 going into Year 11. The bond repayments of $6,600,000 represented the principal payments owed on bonds 1, 2, and 3 (see Note 6 on the Year 10 Balance Sheet). The bond interest payments were for these same three bonds.

Exhibit 7-2

The Cash Flow Report

CASH INFLOWS	
Beginning Cash Balance	0
Receipts from Footwear Sales (see Note 1)	100,077
New Bond Issues	0
New Stock Issues	0
Sale or Liquidation of Plant Capacity	0
Short-Term Loan	0
Cash Refund	0
Total Cash Inflows	100,077
CASH OUTFLOWS	
Payments to Materials Suppliers (see Note 2)	23,520
Operating ————-Production (See Note 3)	27,823
Expenses Warehouse	12,589
Marketing (see Note 4)	12,492
Administrative	3,900
Payments for New Plant Capacity	0
Payments for Plant Automation	0
Payments for New Company-Owned Stores	0
Bond Principal Payments	6,600
Bond Interest Payments	5,735
Repayment of Short-Term Loan	1,030
Short-Term Interest Payment (Income)	98
Common Stock Repurchases	0
Income Tax Payment	3,857
Dividend Payments	2,400
Cash Fines	0
Total Cash Outflows	100,044
NET CASH BALANCE	33

Note 1: Receipts from footwear sales represent 75% of Y10 revenues and 25% of Y9 revenues, due to the three-month lag in receivables collection.

Note 2: Payments to materials suppliers represent 75% of the cost of raw materials used in Y10 and 25% of the cost of raw materials used in Y9, due to a three-month lag in payments to materials suppliers.

Note 3: This number includes all production-related expenses except for depreciation, since depreciation of plant and equipment is a non-cash accounting charge that does not impact current-year cash outflows.

Note 4: This number includes all marketing-related expenses except for depreciation, since depreciation of company-owned store facilities and fixtures is a non-cash accounting charge that does not impact current-year cash outflows.

There are four things you need to bear in mind about the company's cash flows:

- Because the company does not receive payment on many of its online orders made in December and because many retailers do not pay for shipments received after August 1 until the beginning of the following year, the company's cash inflow from footwear sales does not match exactly with annual revenues reported on the Income Statement.[1] Receipts from footwear sales always amount to 25% of prior-year sales plus 75% of current-year sales.

- Cash from bond issues and stock issues is received in the *same year* such issues are made. Cash from the sale of a plant is also received in the same year the sale is negotiated and approved by your instructor/game administrator. Cash from any plant liquidation or closing of company megastores is received in the same year the closing decisions are made.

- The payments for materials, however, consist of 25% of material costs for the previous year plus 75% of material costs for the current year since suppliers are not paid for materials used after October 1 of each year until after January 1.

- It is company practice to pay all income taxes owed during the calendar year so that at year-end it is current on its income tax liabilities; thus, the income tax payments of $3,857,000 represented the full 30% tax owed on Year 10 pre-tax income of $12,857,000. Likewise, the company's full dividend declaration is paid during the calendar year.

The Balance Sheet

Exhibit 7-3 shows your company's Balance Sheet at the end of Year 10. Total assets amounted to $108,682,000, of which $78,000,000 represented investment in the North American and Asian plants. The accounts receivable balance of $25,019,000 represents 25% of Year 10 sales revenues collected in Year 11. The company grants three to five months' credit to independent retailers; many retailers take advantage of this credit policy and do not pay for shipments received after August 1 until the beginning of the following year. Moreover, the company does not receive payment from many online sales made in December during the heavy holiday shopping season until the following year. Current liabilities consist of accounts payable plus short-term loans. The company's one account payable consists of 25% of Year 10 materials purchased from suppliers that do not have to be paid for until January 1 of Year 11 (see Note 3 in Exhibit 7-3); all other expenses incurred in Year 10, including income taxes, are paid no later than the last day of each year and thus do not represent year-end liabilities.

Any short-term loan taken out to help finance company operations shows up as a current liability since the note is due the following year. The accounts payable balance of $5,880,000 represents 25% of Year 10 materials purchases that will be paid for in Year 11. Long-term debt amounts to $43,400,000 and is in the form of three bonds with interest rates, annual principal payments, and interest costs as shown in Note 6. The company has 6 million shares of stock outstanding, as shown in Note 7. Total liabilities going into Year 11 equal $55,880,000 and total stockholders' equity going into Year 11 is $52,802,000.

---

[1] *Company accountants, relying upon generally accepted accounting principles, base income statement revenues on total footwear sales during the calendar year. Actual cash collections from footwear sales do not equal **annual** revenues because payments on footwear ordered and shipped in the last several months of one year are not received until January and February of the following year.*

Exhibit 7-3

The Balance Sheet

ASSETS

Cash On Hand	33	
Accounts Receivable (see Note 1)	25,019	
Footwear Inventories	5,630	
Total Current Assets		30,682
Property, Plant, and ——— Gross Investment	90,000	
Equipment Accumulated Depreciation	12,000	
(see Note 2) Net Investment		78,000
Total Assets		108,682

LIABILITIES AND SHAREHOLDER EQUITY

Accounts Payable (see Note 3)	5,880	
Short-Term Loan Payable (see Note 4)	0	
Current Portion of Long-Term Debt (see Note 5)	6,600	
Total Current Liabilities		12,480
Long-Term Bonds Outstanding (see Note 6)		43,400
Total Liabilities		55,880
Shareholder Equity ——— Common Stock (see Note 7)	6,000	
Additional Shareholder Capital (see Note 8)	30,000	
Accumulated Retained Earnings (see Note 9)	16,802	
Total Shareholder Equity		52,802
Total Liabilities and Shareholder Equity		108,682

Note 1: Of the $100,580 in revenues reported on the Income Statement, 25% have not been collected from customers as of the end of Year 10, and will be collected in Year 11.

Note 2: Property, plant, and equipment represents the company's aggregate investment in plants and company-owned store facilities.

Note 3: Of the $23,520 in materials expenses listed on the Manufacturing Report, 25% have not been paid for as of the end of Year 10, and will be paid for in Year 11.

Note 4: The company qualifies for a short-term interest rate of 9.50%.

Note 5: The current portion of long-term debt is a summation of all principle payments on outstanding bonds that are due to be paid in Year 11.

Note 6: Long-term bonds outstanding:

Bond Number	Year Issued	Original Bond Amount ($000s)	Interest Rate	Outstanding Principle ($000s)	Annual Principle Payment ($000s)	Year 11 Interest Payment ($000s)
1	Year 6	24,000	7.50 %	14,400	2,400	1,080
2	Year 8	22,000	12.50	17,600	2,200	2,200
3	Year 9	20,000	10.00	18,000	2,000	1,800
4						
5						
6						
7						
8						
9						
10						
11						
12						
				50,000	6,600	5,080

Note 7: Common stock carries a par value of $1.00 per share. There are 6,000 (thousand) shares outstanding and a maximum of 50,000 (thousand) shares authorized.

Note 8: Additional shareholder capital is a measure of the amount that shareholders have invested in the company's common stock over and above par value.

Note 9: Accumulated retained earnings is a summation of the after-tax profits the company has earned over all its years of operation that have not been paid out in the form of dividends.

The covenants in the company's bonds outstanding preclude the issue of any new bonds unless the projected times-interest-earned coverage ratio is 2.0 or greater. Hence, to guarantee your company's access to the bond market in the years to come, you and your co-managers will have to monitor the times-interest-earned coverage closely and do everything you can to keep it above 2.0 each year.

The Company's Bond Rating

At present, your company has a bond rating of BBB—a solid rating given the seven ratings that are assigned to footwear companies (AAA, AA, A, BBB, BB, B, and C). Triple-A bonds denote a financially solid company; bonds carrying a C rating are considered "junk bonds." The bond ratings assigned to footwear companies are a function of three factors: (1) the company's debt-to-assets ratio, (2) the times-interest-earned coverage ratio (the number of times which operating profit exceeds annual interest expenses), and (3) the strategic risk factor.

The Debt-Assets Ratio. Your company's debt-to-assets ratio at the end of Year 10 was 0.46 ($50,000,000 in *total* debt divided by assets of $108,682,000). In calculating this ratio, *debt is defined as the sum of long-term bonds outstanding and short-term loans*. A debt-to-asset ratio below 0.25 (or 25%) is considered by bond rating agencies as quite good from a risk and creditworthiness standpoint. However, once the debt-assets ratio reaches 0.50 (or 50%), higher ratios have a progressively negative effect on the company's bond rating. Debt-asset ratios greater than 0.65 will almost certainly result in bond ratings of BB or lower (unless your company has a very strong times-interest-earned coverage ratio to offset the impact of risky debt levels).

The Times-Interest-Earned Coverage Ratio. The times-interest-earned ratio is calculated by dividing companywide operating profit by total interest expenses (both are shown on the Income Statement). In Year 10 your company's times-interest-earned ratio was 3.20 ($18,690,000 ÷ $5,833,000 = 3.20), meaning that the company's operating profits were big enough to cover current interest payment obligations by a factor of 3.2 times. *A coverage ratio of 2.0 is considered minimum* by risk-conscious bondholders and bond buyers because a sudden drop-off in sales or a run-up in operating costs can crimp a company's cash flows and imperil its ability to meet its interest payment obligations. *Should your company's projected time-interest-earned ratio fall below 2.0 in a particular year, the company will be barred from floating a new bond issue.* For example, if the onscreen calculations show that company's *projected* interest coverage ratio will be only 1.8 in the upcoming year, no new bond issue will be allowed—you can, however, utilize a short-term loan for debt financing. In the following year, if the company's projected operating income improves sufficiently and results in a projected times-interest-earned coverage ratio above 2.0, your company will regain access to the bond market. Also, *if your company's projected bond rating falls into the C range, your company may be denied access to further debt even if times-interest-earned is above 2.0* unless stockholders put up additional equity in the form of a new stock issue.

> The debt-to-assets ratio, the times-interest-earned ratio, and the strategic risk factor are the measures used to determine your company's bond rating.

The Strategic Risk Factor. Securities analysts also calculate a "strategic risk factor" as part of their bond rating analysis. The strategic risk factor is a function of (1) how much plant capacity your company has, (2) the percentage of total pairs sold accounted for by private-label sales, and (3) the number of geographic regions in which your company has plants. Your company's risk factor is judged to be greater when

- Your company's plant capacity is "high"—say 10 million pairs or greater. The more plant capacity your company has, the greater the market share you must achieve to attain cost-effective levels of capacity utilization.

- Your company has a "high" percentage of its total sales coming from private-label sales. High levels of private-label sales (say above a 30% of total volume) is considered risky by securities analysts because a company's grip on such sales is relatively weak as is the market share—it is easy for rival companies to steal market share away by simply submitting a lower bid price. The loss of private-label market share can come swiftly, thus impairing a company's operating income, its times-interest-earned coverage ratio, and its ability to meet its debt obligations.

- It has plants in all four regions of the world market, thus making it less subject to tariff increases and exchange rate fluctuations.

A company's risk factor ranges from a low of 1 (least risky) to a high of 10 (most risky). Risk factors greater than 7 have a progressively negative impact on a company's bond rating. Risk factors lower than 7 have a progressively positive impact on a company's bond rating.

Finance and Cash Flow Decisions

Exhibit 7-4 shows the various corporate financing options that you have and the array of supporting calculations you can use to arrive at a satisfactory financing strategy. There are decision entries relating to short-term loans, new bond issues, new stock issues, early bond repayment, stock repurchases, and dividends—the numbers in the boxes represent the Year 10 decisions of prior management. The projected cash flows and the other supporting calculations provided on the screen under the decision entries provide you with the feedback and projected outcomes needed to evaluate the various options you have to finance the company's operations. You can "what-if" any number of financing combinations and use the onscreen calculations to create a financing strategy that holds the potential for the most favorable financial outcomes.

Interest Rates on Bonds and Short-Term Loans. The interest rate the company pays on short-term loans is tied to the current-year prime rate; companies with a AAA bond rating are entitled to short-term loans at the announced prime rate; the interest rate on short-term loans for all other companies is adjusted upward for lower bond ratings, as shown in Exhibit 7-5. There are seven bond ratings, and the interest rate your company pays on new bond issues is tied to the company's current-year bond rating—see the bond interest rate schedule in Exhibit 7-5.

Decisions to Request a Short-Term Loan. The company's agreement with its consortium of global banks states that *management has discretionary authority to borrow any amount on a short-term basis up to $100 million, provided the company's projected bond rating and debt status does not become alarming to creditors.* The interest rate paid on short-term loans is tied to the company's current bond rating; for example, a short-term loan taken out in Year 11 carries an interest rate based on the Year 10 bond rating. Your company currently has a bond rating of BBB; so the interest rate paid on short-term loans will be 9.50% in Year 11. You should expect the prime interest rate to change as the game progresses (perhaps annually); your instructor/game administrator will inform you of any changes in the prime rate for short-term loans.

All short-term loans are repaid the year after they are taken out, but amounts needed to repay prior-year short-term loans can be financed with a new short-term loan at the current year's interest rate. You will need to be careful about the amount of debt your company incurs in the form of long-term bonds and short-term loans. Past a debt-to-assets ratio of 50%, the company's bond rating will start to deteriorate unless the times-interest-earned coverage ratio is high enough to offset the perceived risks to bondholders.

Exhibit 7-4

Finance and Cash Flow Decisions

Decisions: [icons] Reports: FIR [icons] Analysis: [icons] Utility: [icons]

Finance & Cash Flow   Get HELP

Sources of Additional Cash	Request for Short-Term Loan ($000s @ 9.50% annual interest)	$	0
	New Bond Issue ($000s @ 9.50% annual interest)	$	0
	Common Stock Issue (000s of shares @ $13.50 per share)		0
Uses of Available Cash	Early Bond Repayment — Bond Number (see Note 6 of Balance Sheet)		0
	Amount to Repay Early ($000s)	$	0
	Common Stock Retirement (000s of shares @ $18.75 per share)		0
	Dividend Declaration ($ per share)	$	0.40

Projected Cash Flow Report for Year 11 ($000s)

Beginning Cash Balance	$ 33	Cash Outflows	Materials Payments	$ 25704
			Operations	59220
Cash Inflows — Receipts from Footwear Sales	109144		New Capacity / Equipment	0
New Bond Issues	0		New Company-Owned Stores	0
New Stock Issues	0		Bond Principle	6600
Sale or Liquidation of Assets	0		Bond Interest	5735
Short-Term Loan	0		Short-Term Loan Repayment	0
Total Cash Inflows	109144		Short-Term Interest Income	-1
			Stock Repurchases	0
Total Cash Available from All Sources	$ 109177		Income Taxes	4368
			Dividends to Stockholders	2400
Accumulated Retained Earnings Balance (projected) $ 21078			Total Cash Outflows	$ 104026

| Shares = 6000 | Debt-To-Assets = 0.41 | Times-Interest-Earned = 4.59 | Strategic Risk Factor = 3 | Bond Rating = BBB |
| Sales Revenues = $112,166 | Net Profit = $10,193 | EPS = $1.70 | ROI = 15.85% | Cash Balance = $5,151 |

The Business Strategy Game — 7th Edition , © 2001 McGraw-Hill/Irwin   ↑ ↓   If necessary, click arrows to adjust screen to best fit.

Decisions Regarding Bond Issues. All bonds are issued for a 10-year term. The principal on 10-year bonds is repaid annually in equal installments; interest on the outstanding principal is paid annually. The interest rate on each long-term bond issue is based on the company's bond rating as of the prior year—in other words, a bond issued in Year 12 carries an interest rate based on the Year 11 bond rating. Your company currently has a bond rating of BBB, so the interest rate paid on a new issue in Year 11 will be 9.50% (as per the schedule in Exhibit 7-5). You should expect the interest rate on AAA bonds to change as the game progresses (perhaps annually); your instructor/game administrator will inform you of any changes in the AAA bond rate. *Your company is limited to a maximum of 12 bond issues (3 of which have already been used up by prior management) and to a maximum of $99,999,000 per new bond issue.*

The covenants in the company's bonds outstanding preclude the issue of any new bonds unless the projected times-interest-earned coverage ratio for the upcoming year is 2.0 or greater. Hence, to guarantee your company's access to the bond market in the years to come, you and your co-managers will have to monitor the times-interest-earned coverage closely and do everything you can to keep it above 2.0 each year. Consequently, *you and your co-managers are well advised to observe prudent financial management practices and avoid excessive reliance on debt financing. In the event that your company is blocked*

To qualify for a new bond issue, your company's times-interest-earned ratio must exceed 2.0 in the year preceding a new issue.

from the bond market, you will still have access to short-term loans. Indeed, if your company's bond rating falls to B or C thus resulting in high interest rates on any new bond issues, you and your co-managers should consider using short-term loans for any debt-financing needs and wait to issue long-term bonds when your bond rating improves and the interest rate declines. Issuing a long-term bond at a high interest rate locks the company in to high annual interest charges for a 10-year period; while in later years you may be able to prepay a long-term bond carrying a high interest rate and refinance the outstanding principal at lower interest rates, the 2% prepayment penalty on bonds usually makes it more economical to use short-term loans to cover borrowing needs whenever the company has low bond ratings.

Exhibit 7-5

Interest Rates and Adjustment Factors

Current Year Bond Rating	Interest Rate on New Bond Issues	Interest Rate on Short-Term Loans
AAA	7.50%* or as announced	Prime rate of 7.50%* (or as announced)
AA	AAA rate plus 0.50%	Prime rate plus 0.50%
A	AAA rate plus 1.25%	Prime rate plus 1.25%
BBB	AAA rate plus 2.00%	Prime rate plus 2.00%
BB	AAA rate plus 3.00%	Prime rate plus 3.00%
B	AAA rate plus 5.00%	Prime rate plus 5.00%
C	AAA rate plus 8.00%	Prime rate plus 8.00%

* The 7.5% rate will prevail for future years unless modified in some fashion described by your instructor/game administrator.

The methodology used by securities analysts to assess the company's debt-assets ratio, times-interest-earned coverage ratio, and risk factor and thus determine company bond ratings is programmed on the company disk, allowing you to obtain projections of the bond rating based on current year decisions and projected company performance—see the next-to-last line in the calculations section on the Finance and Cash Flow Decisions screen. As you and your co-managers make decisions about both short-term loans and new bond issues, you should pay close attention to the calculations showing your company's debt-assets ratio, the times-interest-earned ratio, and the risk factor—all of which affect your company's bond rating and the interest rates you will pay on future-year borrowings. Protecting your company's creditworthiness and ability to borrow at attractive interest rates is particularly crucial if your strategy requires new capital for expansion or if your company needs to refinance high-interest debt to escape burdensome interest costs. See Exhibit 7-6 at the end of this section for explanations of the key financial ratios used in *The Business Strategy Game*.

Decisions to Issue New Shares of Common Stock. It is very likely in financing the company's growth that additional shares of common stock will have to be issued. Investor interest in the company has been high enough that you can count on being able to sell additional shares and raise new equity capital. *New shares of common stock are issued at the prevailing market price less a discount based on the percentage dilution.* For example, issuing 10% more shares will entail an issue price per new share roughly 10% below the prevailing price appearing in the most recent issue of the Footwear Industry Report. *When you enter the number of shares (in thousands) to be issued, the discounted issue price will be displayed beside the new common stock issue entry.* The following example takes you through the cash flow and balance sheet implications of stock issues:

Assume the company decides to raise capital by issuing 1 million shares of stock and that the discounted issue price is $12 per share. The 1 million-share stock issue will then generate $12 million in cash (1 million shares × $12 per share) for immediate use. In the stockholders' equity portion of the balance sheet, the Common Stock account will increase by $1 million ($1 par value × 1 million shares issued), and the Additional Stockholders' Capital account will increase by $11 million [($12 issue price—$1 par value) × 1 million shares issued].

Early Bond Repayment Decisions. You can retire all or part of any outstanding bonds early, but there is a 2% prepayment penalty on the early retirement amount. To use the early bond payment decision option, simply enter the bond number (1 through 12; see Note 6 on the balance sheet) that you wish to make an *extra* payment on, and enter the amount of the *extra* payment (in thousands of dollars). The 2% prepayment penalty will be calculated by the computer immediately upon an early bond repayment entry, and automatically charged to bond interest for the year. *It makes sense to consider refinancing high-interest bonds at lower interest rates whenever such refinancing will lower the company's overall interest expenses* (taking into account the 2% prepayment cost).

Common Stock Retirement Decisions. If you wish to retire outstanding shares by repurchasing them from investors, then you may buy them back at a price that escalates above the prevailing price according to percentage of shares being retired. In other words, *stock buybacks drive up the price of the remaining shares; the bigger the buyback, the higher the repurchase price*. When you enter the number of shares (in thousands) to be repurchased on the screen, the computer will display a message indicating the buyback price beside the common stock retirement entry. The costs of repurchasing shares of the company's common stock can be paid for by using cash on hand, taking out short-term loans, issuing a new bond, or even cutting the dividend. However, the Board of Directors has decreed that the company will have no fewer than 3 million shares outstanding; hence, *you cannot repurchase shares in an amount that will bring the number of shares outstanding below 3 million shares*. The following example explains the cash flow and balance sheet implications of stock retirement:

Assume the company decides to retire 1 million shares of outstanding stock at a buyback price of $18.50. The 1 million-share stock retirement will require $18.5 million in cash ($18.50 per share × 1 million shares retired). In the stockholders' equity section of the balance sheet, the Common Stock account will decrease by $1 million ($1 par value × 1 million shares retired) and the Additional Stockholders' Capital account will decrease by $17.5 million [($18.50 repurchase price—$1 par value) × 1 million shares retired].

Once the Additional Stockholders' Capital account balance reaches zero, company accountants treat the cost of stock repurchases as a deduction from Retained Earnings (except for the $1 par value deducted from the Common Stock account). *The cost of shares repurchased cannot result in negative retained earnings. Once the amount of accumulated retained earnings on the balance sheet reaches zero, all further stock repurchases will be automatically denied.*[2]

Dividends. The size of the company's annual dividend is a significant matter to stockholders, especially the three co-founders who depend on their annual dividend checks as a primary source of income. Increases or decreases in the dividend are reflected immediately in the stock price. It is your decision henceforth whether to continue the present $0.40 annual dividend, whether to raise it, or whether to cut it.

---

[2] *Retained earnings are **not** cash and cannot be used to pay for anything. The accumulated retained earnings amount shown on the balance sheet is no more than an accounting summation of the after-tax profits the company has earned over all its years of operation that have not been paid out to stockholders in the form of dividends.*

In Year 10, the company earned $1.50 per share after taxes and paid out $0.40 per share in dividends. With total earnings of $9,000,000 and total dividend payments of $2,400,000 ($0.40 per share × 6,000,000 shares outstanding), it follows that both accumulated retained earnings and total stockholders' equity in Year 10 increased by $6,600,000. If you declare a dividend that is higher than the current year's earnings, the accumulated retained earnings balance (and also total stockholders' equity) will decrease. *Under no circumstances will you be allowed to declare a dividend if the company's accumulated retained earnings balance is negative or a dividend that would cause the company's accumulated retained earnings balance to become negative.* Otherwise, the Board of Directors will approve whatever decision you recommend on dividends.

Interest Rate Paid on Cash Balances. The company's banking arrangements call for the company to be paid interest on any positive cash balance in the company's checking account at the beginning of each year. The agreed-upon interest rate is set at three percentage points below the prevailing prime interest rate. At present (unless announced otherwise), the prime rate is 7.5%; thus the money market rate paid on cash balances is 4.5%. If you and your co-managers should at any time fail to maintain a year-end cash balance of zero or greater, the banks will automatically issue your company a short-term loan in an amount sufficient to bring your checking account balance up to zero. The interest rate charged on the *entire amount of short-term borrowing that year* will be *2% above the regular rate*. In other words, if your bond rating entitles your company to a short-term interest rate of 8.25%, then the penalty rate of an automatic bank loan would be 10.25% on the entire loan amount. Overdrawing your checking account is costly and should be avoided.

> Computer-generated short-term loans carry a 2% interest rate penalty over and above the regular interest rate.

Factors Affecting the Company's Stock Price. At the end of Year 10, your company's stock price was $15 per share. Whether your company's stock price goes up or down as the game progresses is a function of:

1. *The company's revenue growth* (as measured by the compound growth rate of revenues since Year 10)—Faster rates of revenue growth tend to push the stock price up.

2. *The 3-year trend in the company's earnings per share*—Investors have decided that the growth trend in the company's earnings growth is best reflected by the year-to-year change in the 3-year average of earnings per share. An increase in the 3-year moving average has a positive impact on the stock price; a lower 3-year moving average has a negative impact on the stock price.

3. *The annual rate of return earned on net investment (ROI)*—Higher rates of return on investment signal a more profitable use of investors' capital and have a positive impact on the stock price. ROI is defined as net income plus interest payments on debt divided by stockholders' equity plus total debt—in effect, ROI represents the "return on capital employed" since it includes the net income received by stockholders for the equity capital they have contributed and the interest payments to bondholders and the company's banks for whatever debt capital they have provided. In Year 10, the company had net income of $9,000,000, interest payments on debt of $5,833,000, stockholders' equity of $52,802,000, and total debt of $50,000, equal to an ROI of 14.4%.

4. *The 3-year trend in ROI*—Investor confidence in the company is boosted when the company's 3-year average ROI is rising. An increase in the 3-year moving

average ROI has a positive impact on the stock price; a lower 3-year moving average has a negative impact on the stock price.

5. ***Earnings per share growth*** (as measured by the compound growth rate of earnings per share since Year 10)—faster rates of EPS growth tend to push the stock price up and slower or negative rates pull it down. Thus whether EPS has increased, decreased, or remained unchanged compared to the Year 10 level of $1.50 per share will affect the stock price. The co-founders and investors have strong views about the importance of EPS increasing steadily over Year 10 levels.

Your company's stock price is a function of 9 factors.

6. ***Growth in the annual dividend*** (as measured by the compound growth rate of dividends since Year 10)—faster rates of dividend growth tend to push the stock price up and slower (or negative) rates pull it down. Thus whether the dividend has increased, decreased, or remained unchanged compared to the Year 10 level of $0.40 per share will affect the stock price.

7. Whether ***the company's dividend payout ratio*** (defined as current dividends per share as a percentage of current earnings per share) exceeds 100%—Paying a dividend that exceeds EPS has a depressing effect on the stock price, since it impairs cash flow and is unsustainable.

8. ***The company's bond rating***—higher bond ratings have a positive effect on the stock price because they signal a stronger financial condition.

9. ***The strategic risk factor***—lower risk factors have a positive stock price effect because they signal less business risk.

Of these nine factors, the EPS growth as compared against the Year value of $1.50 per share, the annual ROI, and the 3-year moving averages in both EPS and ROI have the biggest impact on stock price. The dividend payout ratio has virtually no impact ***unless*** the company fails to earn the dividend and the payout ratio exceeds 100%. The other four factors influencing the company's stock price are of varying intermediate importance.

Exhibit 7-6
Key Financial Ratios and Performance Measures

Ratio	Calculation	Meaning / Why It Is Important
Debt-Assets Ratio	$\dfrac{\text{Total Debt (Bonds and S-T Loans)}}{\text{Total Assets}}$	Measures the extent to which borrowed funds have been used to finance the firm's operations. Affects the company's bond rating.
Times-Interest-Earned Ratio	$\dfrac{\text{Operating Profit}}{\text{Total Interest Payments}}$	Measures the extent to which earnings can decline without the firm becoming unable to cover its annual interest costs. Affects bond rating.
Return on Investment (or return on capital employed)	$\dfrac{\text{Net Income + Interest Expense}}{\text{Capital Employed}}$	Measures the return on capital invested by both creditors and stockholders. Capital employed = total debt + stockholders' equity.
Earnings Per Share (EPS)	$\dfrac{\text{Net Income}}{\text{No. of Shares Outstanding}}$	Shows the earnings available to the owners of each share of stock. EPS directly affects the company's stock price and the year-end score.
Dividend Payout Ratio	$\dfrac{\text{Dividends Per Share}}{\text{Earnings Per Share}}$	Indicates the percentage of annual profits distributed to common share holders. Affects the company's' stock price.
Days of Inventory	$\dfrac{\text{Ending Inventory (units)}}{\text{Total Unit Sales}} \times 365$	Shows how long the current inventory would last into the upcoming year, assuming the same annual unit sales as the previous year.

Scoring, Reports, Analysis Options, and Strategic Plans

This section explains how company performance is scored, gives you a bird's-eye view of the industry and company reports generated after each decision, and describes the built-in analysis and planning tools the software gives you, including the important three-year strategic planning option. After you turn in the Company Data Disk with your decisions on it, the instructor/game administrator will process all the company decisions and return the disk to you with the year's financial results and actual competitive outcomes. On the disk you'll find three key industry reports—the Footwear Industry Report (which features a scoreboard of company performances and an array of industry and competitive information), the Benchmarking Report, and two competitor analysis reports. You'll also be able to review each of the eight company reports and see what actually occurred for the year in all phases of company operations. Finally, there's a series of analysis and strategic planning options to help you and you co-managers diagnose industry and competitive conditions and to prepare a strategic plan that looks three years down the road.

Scoring Your Company's Performance

The Industry Scoreboard is the lead section in each year's issue of the Footwear Industry Report. The scoreboard section provides a rundown of each company's relative standing on revenues, after-tax earnings and earnings per share, return on investment, bond rating, market capitalization (stock price multiplied by the number of shares outstanding), and strategy rating. These six performance measures, as a group, are the basis for judging your company's overall performance and determining your company's position in the industry rankings. If your company leads the industry in revenues from footwear sales, then your company will earn a score of 100 on the revenue component of performance. If your company is not the revenue leader, your company's score on the revenue component equals whatever percent your company's revenue is of the leader's revenue. For instance, if your company has revenues of $80 million versus $100 million for the industry's revenue leader, then your company's score on the revenue component of overall performance will be 80 (since your company's revenues are 80% of those of the company with the highest revenues).

Your company's performance scores on earnings per share (or EPS), return on investment (ROI), market capitalization (defined at your company's latest stock price multiplied by the number of shares of stock outstanding), and strategy rating are computed in similar fashion. If your company is the industry leader on any of these performance measures, your company's score is 100; otherwise your company's score equals whatever *percentage* of the industry leader's performance your company achieves. However, in the case of after-tax earnings (or EPS) and return on equity, it is possible that some companies will lose money and have a negative return on equity; the scores of money-losing companies for profits and ROI are set at zero. If all companies in the industry incur after-tax losses and/or have negative returns on equity investment, then all companies get scores of 0 on these two performance measures.

Scoring in *The Business Strategy Game* is based on how your company performs relative to rival companies on six measures:

- **Sales Revenues**
- **Earnings Per Share (EPS)**
- **Return on Investment (ROI)**
- **Bond Rating**
- **Market Capitalization**
- **Strategy Rating**

The financial community refers to the total dollar value of all the shares a company has outstanding as the company's "market capitalization." In effect, market capitalization represents the total dollar value that investors have placed on the company. The company with the highest market capitalization (and thus the highest investor rating) earns a perfect score on this performance measure. Every other company's score is calculated as a percentage of the leader's market capitalization. If your company's market capitalization is $120 million and the leader's is $150 million, then your company's score on the market capitalization performance measure will be 80 (because your company's value is 80% of the highest valued company). *Scoring is thus based on relative company performance rather than industry rank.* The company with the best performance on each of the five measures (revenues, earnings, ROI, market capitalization, and strategy rating) earns a perfect score of 100 on that measure; the scores of all other companies are calculated as a percent of the leader's performance.

Performance scores on bond ratings are calculated a bit differently. An AAA rating (the highest) carries a score of 100 and a C bond rating (the lowest) carries a score of 0.

The scores for the five ratings between AAA and C fall in between the two extremes: an AA rating is scored as 90, an A rating equals 80, a BBB rating equals 60, a BB rating equals 40, and a B rating carries a score of 20.

How the Strategy Rating Is Calculated. The strategy rating is designed to measure and rank the "power" of each company's strategy and the distinctiveness with which the company's footwear stands apart from that of rivals on the basis of some relevant attribute. The intent is to reward companies that develop distinctive strategies to (1) stake out a particular position in the marketplace, (2) build a sustainable competitive advantage of one kind or another, and (3) develop a reputation with consumers as an industry leader on one or more product attributes or competitive factors. The higher a company's strategy rating, the more its strategy or its footwear products "stand out" in the industry.

The Strategy Rating does not assess "how good" a company's strategy is; rather, it measures what a company is known for and how much a company stands apart from rivals.

Exhibit 8-1 describes the point system used in calculating strategy ratings. A listing of how many strategy rating points each company has earned on each power measure is reported in each year's Footwear Industry Report. Companies with the biggest number of strategy rating points on the power measures shown in Exhibit 8-1 possess some element of competitive advantage; companies with few strategy rating points generally are "stuck in the middle" or suffer from competitive disadvantage.

Overall Company Performance Scores. Your company's overall performance score is a *weighted average* of the scores on the six individual performance measures—sales revenues, after-tax profits (or EPS), ROI, market capitalization, bond rating, and strategy rating. The instructor or game administrator will announce the weights to be placed on each measure. The overall score your company receives relative to the scores of rival companies indicates how well your company is doing. For example, if the highest score of any company is 90 and your company's overall score is 60, then your company is doing two-thirds as well as the industry leader—which is not terrible but which leaves ample room for improvement. *The highest possible overall score is 100.* To obtain a score of 100, a company must be the best performing company on all six measures. An overall score in the 90s is excellent; an overall score in the 80s is very good. An overall score of 40 signals a need for serious strategy review and performance improvement.

Game-to-Date Performance. The Industry Scoreboard section shows not only the company standings for the immediately concluded year but also game-to-date company standings (all years combined, starting with Year 11). The game-to-date scores are based on *cumulative* revenues, *cumulative* after-tax profits, the overall game-to-date return on investment, current-year market capitalization, the latest bond rating, and the average strategy rating for the last three years. (Thus at the end of the game it is your company's three most recent strategy ratings that count in the overall standings, not the strategy ratings that the company used to have early in the game.)

The highest possible overall game-to-date score is 100; to obtain it, a company must be the industry leader on all six performance measures. As with current year scores, an overall game-to-date score in the 90s is excellent; a score in the 80s is very good. *The two themes underlying the entire scoring procedure are that (1) standard yardsticks of business performance are utilized, and (2) each company's performance is judged relative to how well other companies in the industry have done.*

Exhibit 8-1

Strategy Rating Point System

Strategy Criteria	How Measured	Points Earned
Broad/Focused Product Line	To qualify as "broad" or "focused", a company's weighted average number of models available in a branded region must be at least 20% **above** or **below** the region average.	1 point for each 10% that the company's weighted average number of models available in a branded region is above or below the region average (maximum of 10 points per region).
High Quality	To qualify as "high", a company's quality rating in a branded region must be at least 20 points **above** the region average.	1 point for each 10 points that the company's quality rating in a branded region exceeds the region average (maximum of 10 points per region).
Good Service	To qualify as "good", a company's service rating in a branded region must be at least 20 points **above** the region average.	1 point for each 10 points that the company's service rating in a branded region exceeds the region average (maximum of 10 points per region).
Brand Image	A company's brand image stands out when its image rating in a branded region is at least 20 points **above** the region average.	1 point for each 10 points that the company's image rating in a branded region exceeds the region average (maximum of 10 points per region).
Low Overall Cost	To qualify as "low cost", a company's operating costs per pair sold must be at least 10% **below** the average for branded regions or at least 2% **below** the private-label average.	1 point for each 2% that the company's operating cost per pair sold is below the average in a branded region or in the private-label segment.
Market Share Leadership	A company is designated a "market share leader" when its sales volume in a branded region, on the Internet, or in the private-label segment is at least 15% **above** the region/segment average. The degree of leadership depends on how much the average is exceeded.	1 point for each 5% that the company's market share is above the average market share of branded sales in a geographic region or on the Internet or in the private label segment.
Superior Value	A company's product is considered to be of "superior value" when its value-price ratio in a branded region and/or on the Internet is at least 10% **above** the region average. The value-price ratio is calculated as follows: $$\frac{\text{Quality Rating} + \text{Number of Models}}{\text{Selling Price}}$$	1 point for each 3% that the company's value-price ratio in a branded region exceeds the region average or the global average in the case of sales via the Internet. No points are awarded in the private-label segment because price alone is the decisive competitive variable.
Global/Focused Coverage	To qualify for "global" market coverage, a company must derive a minimum of 10% of its total branded sales volume from **each** region. To qualify for "focused" market coverage, a company must derive at least 50% of its total branded sales volume from a **single** region or from the private-label segment.	10 points for achieving minimal global coverage, plus 1 point for each percent that a company's total branded sales volume exceeds 10% in each of the four geographic regions. 10 points for focused coverage, plus 1 point for each percent that a company's branded sales volume exceeds 50% in a single geographic region.

Special Note: *A company must sell at least 100,000 pairs in a geographic region to qualify for strategy rating points in that region.*

Judging company performance on a ***relative*** rather than an ***absolute*** basis is much sounder and fairer than rankings based on which company is in "first place" and which is in "last place". A company that is in last place with an overall performance score of 70 is plainly doing much better than a company in last place with an overall score of 25. In an industry of 10 companies, some company must rank tenth, but a tenth-place company with a relative performance score of 70 is obviously a more solid performer than a tenth-place company with a performance score of 25. Hence, it makes far more sense to base grading on a relative overall performance score than on absolute industry rankings.

The Footwear Industry Report

You can see what the industry scoreboard looks like by clicking on the Footwear Industry Report button on the Menu Bar. *Your instructor will determine the weights placed on each performance measure.* Very likely, your instructor will rely heavily on your company's overall game-to-date performance score in determining the grade you and your co-managers receive on *The Business Strategy Game* exercise.

Following the Industry Scoreboard is a second section of the Footwear Industry Report containing industry-wide information on total revenues and total pairs sold in each geographic market, year-end inventories, capacity utilization, materials prices, and a five-year demand forecast. Then there's a third section providing company-by-company details on the results of private-label bidding, prices charged, pairs sold, stockouts, quality and service ratings, numbers of retailers, advertising, brand image number of models in the product line, rebate programs, and assorted financial and operating statistics. The Footwear Industry Report concludes with a news bulletin announcing special developments, changes in costs or rates, and other matters of interest.

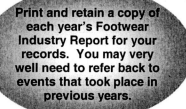
Print and retain a copy of each year's Footwear Industry Report for your records. You may very well need to refer back to events that took place in previous years.

The Five-Year Demand Forecast. Each issue of the Footwear Industry Report contains a forecast of footwear demand for each of the next five years for private-label footwear in North America, branded sales in North America, branded sales in Europe, branded sales in Asia, and branded sales in Latin America. Each year's forecast is in terms of the total number of pairs that can be sold in each segment (to obtain the number of pairs which can be sold by each company *on average*, divide the forecasted amounts by the number of companies in your industry). Be aware, though, that while the demand forecast is reliable in the sense of being based on the latest information and conditions available, it is not an absolute given. As mentioned earlier, demand forecasts in the Footwear Industry Report are subject to future changes in the S&P 500 Index and to unusually strong or weak efforts on the part of the industry to capture the potential demand. Thus, actual sales in any one particular year could, in the extreme, deviate from the forecast by as much as 10% to 15% should there be significant swings in the S&P 500 and should industry efforts to capture the sales potentials prove unusually aggressive or unusually weak.

The first issue of the Footwear Industry Report (FIR) will appear at the end of Year 11, so in making a decision for Year 11 you will not need to review the FIR (the screens will contain zeros). Except for Year 11, the first thing you should normally do when you get your Company Data Disk back with the year's happenings on it is to look at the FIR—*always make a printout of the information it contains and retain it in your records.*

The Benchmarking Report

The Benchmarking Report is a one-page statistical compilation showing how your company stacks up on materials costs, labor costs, reject rates, plant supervision costs, and manufacturing costs—the format of this report can be reviewed by clicking the Benchmarking Report button on the Menu Bar. This report provides cost comparisons for all North American, Asian, European, and Latin American plants. Also it lists how what the high, low, and average costs per pair were in each market segment—private-label and branded (North America, Europe, Asia, and Latin America). Using this information, you can compare the information in your company's cost analysis report to see where your company ranks relative to the company with the highest cost, the company with the lowest costs and the industry average. The Benchmarking Report thus allows you to easily gauge your company's cost competitiveness and see exactly where your company has a cost advantage or disadvantage and what the size of the advantage or disadvantage may be.

The Competitor Analysis Reports

Two types of competitor analysis reports are available—one comparing the competitive efforts of each company in a given year and one that tracks the competitive effort of any company over time. The Competitor Strategy Comparisons Report shows how your company stacks up against rivals on each market share determinant in each of the four market segments—a sample format can be viewed by clicking the button for this report on the Menu Bar. How many branded pairs your company sells is a function of how your company's price, product quality, advertising effort, and so on compares against rivals'. The report makes it easy to compare one company's average price, quality, model availability, service, advertising, retail network, image rating, and rebates against other companies and against the industry averages; these differences indicate who has how big a competitive advantage or disadvantage on each competitive measure, market by market. Such comparisons account for the sales and market share differences across companies and serve as a valuable guide in adjusting your competitive effort to obtain the targeted sales volume in the upcoming year.

The Company Tracking Report provides a year-by-year rundown on the prices, quality ratings, service ratings, advertising, rebates and so on for any rival company of interest. This report highlights the competitive changes a company has made each year in each geographic market, thus giving you a historical data base on which to make judgments about the moves they may make in the upcoming year. After 3 or 4 decision periods, you will find that some rivals are closer competitors than others. *Printing out copies of the tracking report for these close competitors is the quickest and most accurate way to get a scouting report on key rivals*—all the figures in this report come from information appearing in prior issues of the Footwear Industry Report. You can also print out a tracking report for your own company to review the competitive maneuvers that have been undertaken, see which were most successful in terms of pairs sold and market share, and spot where improvements are needed.

Company Reports of Current-Year Results

When the Company Data Disk is returned, you'll be able to either view or obtain printouts of all the company reports detailing the results of operations for the past year. *Ideally, you should print out a full set of company reports*—the manufacturing report, warehouse and sales report, marketing and administrative report, geographic profit report, cost report, income statement, year-end balance sheet, and cash flow report—*for each co-manager. Always retain at least one printout of the entire set of company reports in your records*—you will *not* be able to go back later and obtain the results of earlier years because the results of each new decision are written over the results of prior years.

The Analysis Options

On the Menu Bar are three buttons that provide tools for special analysis:

- A capacity expansion analysis screen that helps you evaluate the profitability of adding new production capacity.

- A Strategic Plan Program.

- A tool for creating charts, graphs, and strategic group maps.

The Capacity Expansion Analysis Option. This screen allows you to explore the profitability of investing in new production capacity—either building a new plant or expanding an existing plant in one or more geographic regions of the world. You are strongly urged to use this analysis option before undertaking any new investments in production capacity. It is unwise to "shoot from the hip" and spending millions on new capacity if there is not a reasonable prospect of satisfactory profitability and return on investment.

The capacity expansion analysis screen contains a number of "what-if" entries regarding a possible investment in new capacity. There's a series of on-screen calculations to help you evaluate the potential profitability of additional capacity, given the what-if entries you've made about plant's operations and likely costs. You'll find that it takes about 10-20 minutes to do an analysis of whether additional capacity has promise for acceptable profitability. It is time well spent, given the hit your company can take on lower performance should the investment not work out. In the "real world" company managers do not spend millions on new plant capacity without some supporting analysis that the investment will improve company performance.

The Strategic Plan Option. One of the most important menu selections on your Company Data Disk is the 3-Year Strategic Plan option. It allows you to build a three-year production plan for each plant, a three-year marketing plan for each market segment (private-label, North America, Europe, Asia, and Latin America), and a three-year financial plan. This menu option contains assorted entry screens, each with revenue-cost-profit projections and other calculations at the bottom to guide the tentative decisions and strategic course you chart. When you complete the plan, you can obtain a printout summarizing the outcomes and performance you can expect from the long-range strategy you've laid out. You'll find the 3-year planning option especially valuable in diagnosing weaknesses in your strategy, checking out the long-term consequences of particular actions (expanding a plant, issuing additional stock, taking on more debt, undertaking various plant upgrade options, and so on), and seeing whether your company's performance is likely to improve or worsen in the years ahead.

Don't be surprised if your instructor/game administrator asks you to prepare at least one 3-year strategic plan as the game progresses. While you may not welcome such an assignment, the fact is that *making decisions one year at a time, with little or no view towards the future and few clues as to the longer-run consequences of current-year decisions, is no way to manage*. In practice, companies put considerable effort into trying to anticipate future market conditions, developing long-range strategies, and making multiyear financial projections because it enhances the quality of managerial decisions. For the same reason, you and your co-managers will find it worthwhile to go through the exercise of developing a three-year plan. Spending some quality time utilizing the 3-year strategic plan feature will give you good insights into how to improve your company's long-term competitive position and financial performance in the years ahead.

The Charts and Graphs Option. This analysis option gives you instantly available data from the Competitor Analysis Report and selected information from the Footwear Industry Report; these enable you to quickly and easily construct an assortment of pie charts, bar graphs, and line graphs. These charts and graphs can help you and your co-managers diagnose industry and company trends and better understand the dynamics of competition in the footwear market.

One of the most valuable tools in this section is the option to construct strategic group maps showing the market positions of various companies in each of the different market segments. As you may have learned from your strategic management text, a strategic group map is a two-dimensional diagram showing which rival firms have similar competitive approaches and positions in the market. Companies in the same strategic group can resemble one another in any of several ways: they may have a comparable number of models and styles, sell in the same price/quality range, emphasize the same distribution channels, place comparable emphasis on customer service, or compete on the basis of a strong brand image. Competition in a particular geographic regions consists of only one strategic group when all sellers are pursuing essentially identical strategies and have comparable market positions (a rather unlikely condition). At the other extreme, there are as many strategic groups as there are competitors when each rival pursues a distinctively different competitive approach and occupies a substantially different competitive position in the marketplace (a rare condition as well). Usually, competition in a geographic region will consist of several strategic groups—some rivals closely grouped perhaps because of their use of a low price and broad product line to attract patronage, others grouped because of a common emphasis on high levels of service and use of retail dealers, and still others grouped because of their competitive reliance on high price/quality and premium scrvice.

The strategic group mapping option already contains a blank map and company circles (sized proportionally based on market share) for you to use. All you have to do is select any two competitive variables as axes for a strategic group map and use the mouse to move the various companies to the appropriate location on the map. You can thus create strategic group maps showing the position of rival companies in North America, Asia, Europe, and Latin America in a matter of a few minutes. You'll find such maps valuable in understanding which rivals are your company's closest competitors and what the pattern of competition is in each region of the world market.

The options you have to construct graphs and charts are particularly useful in preparing an industry and competitve analysis of the global footwear market (which your instructor may require) and in preparing a written strategic plan for your company (which your instructor may also require). Even if you are not required to make use of the analysis tools in this section, you and your co-managers will find these capabilities useful in enhancing your understanding of the competition your company faces and in diagnosing the strategies of rival companies. We urge you to explore and make use of the charts and graphs option on the Menu Bar.

Decision Making: Recommended Procedures

Each year you make decisions for your company, we recommend that you and your co-managers go through the following procedure:

Step 1: Make a printout of the Footwear Industry Report (you can skip this step in making the Year 11 decision since the first FIR issue appears with the Year 11 results). Having a hard copy of this report to consult as you make each new decision is virtually essential. *Keep the printout* so that you can refer back to the information later if need be.

Step 2: Make a printout of the Benchmarking Report. (You should also skip this step for the first decision—the first issue of the Benchmarking Report will be available *after* the Year 11 results have been provided to you.)

Step 3: Beginning with the Year 12, make a printout of the Competitor Strategy Comparisons for Year 11 (you will need at least one copy of this every year). You may also wish to print selected Company Tracking Reports for any company of interest. The more you and your co-managers study the actions of key competitors and are able to anticipate their moves, the better you will be prepared to counter their strategies with offensive and defensive moves of your own.

Step 4: Print out copies of all eight company reports (six pages) and then review them line-by-line to see your company's actual results, financial performance, and operating performance for the past year. The really key reports are the Manufacturing Report, the Warehouse Operations Report, the Cost Analysis, Report and the Geographic Profit Analysis Report. *It is perilous to rush into making decisions for the upcoming year without first having a good command of the prior year results and the strengths and weaknesses of your company's situation.* See how your company compares on each of the items in the Benchmarking Report. Ideally, all company managers should have a copy of the company reports. You should keep one copy in your files in case you have to refer back to these results later.

Step 5: After you have reviewed the Footwear Industry Report, the Benchmarking Report, the Competitor Analysis reports, and the eight company reports, you are ready to begin the decision-making process for the upcoming year. You should start with the Demand Forecast Screen (the first button on the decisions side of the Menu Bar). Make a complete trial decision by going through all the entries on the Demand Forecast Screen and the nine decision screens. Use the information in the industry and company reports and the on-screen calculations to guide your decisions for the upcoming year. Cycle through the various decision screens and the Demand Forecast Screen as many times as you wish—you will find that some cycling back and forth is essential.

Step 6: Make it a point to experiment with alternative actions and strategies—you can cycle back through the decision screens and Demand Forecast Screen, doing as much what-ifing and trying out as many different strategy options and decision combinations as you deem useful. The on-screen calculations and the Demand Forecast Screen make it easy to explore the effects of higher/lower selling prices, a stronger/weaker marketing effort, more/less production, different shipping combinations, different financial approaches, and alternative sales and what-if estimates. Fine-tune your decision entries and demand forecast estimates until you arrive at a course of action that holds promise in producing attractive short-term and long-term outcomes. We strongly urge that you *make regular use the Demand Forecast Screen* to determine what combination of prices and marketing efforts it is likely to take to achieve the desired sales volume in each geographic market—learning to use this screen wisely is time well spent.

Step 7: As you near a final decision, review your company's projected operating reports and financial statements for the upcoming year (by clicking the Company Reports button on the Menu Bar). It is an especially good idea to compare the information in the projected Cost Analysis Report against last year's actual Cost Analysis Report and Benchmarking Report to see if any of the itemized cost projections are significantly higher/lower than the previous year. This gives you a yardstick to measure whether your company's cost-efficiency is getting better or worse. Check the Geographic Profit Analysis Report against last year's Geographic Profit Analysis Report to see if projected profits by area are improving or declining compared to last year. If needed, return to the Demand Forecast Screen and the various decision screens to make further adjustments. Otherwise, *print a copy of the projected Company Reports for your records.*

Step 8: When all of your decision entries and projected outcomes look satisfactory, simply click on the Print button in the Menu Bar at the top of any decision screen (or at the top of the Menu Bar Guide Screen). *Make two printouts of your final decision entries* for the upcoming year. Turn in one copy with your Company Disk and keep the other copy for your records. *Check the printout carefully to be sure, once again, that all your decision entries are as you want them.* Then *exit the program by clicking on the Exit button at the top right of the Menu Bar on any screen; the program automatically saves all of your data and entries to your Company Disk.*

Special Note: *Do not remove the Company Disk from the drive until you have exited completely from The Business Strategy Game using the Exit button.*

Step 9: Submit your Company Disk containing your final decision along with a printout of your final decision to your instructor/game administrator by the agreed-upon time. The year's results will be processed and your Company Disk returned to you, usually no later than the next day, with the actual company results and updated industry reports on it.

Concluding Comments

To do well in *The Business Strategy Game*, you and your co-managers will need to be shrewd analysts of the industry and competitive situation, and you will need to manage internal operations efficiently. We urge you to make full use of the information in the Footwear Industry Report, the Benchmarking Report, the Competitor Analysis reports, and the company reports, and become a conscientious student of what's happening inside and outside your company. You can't expect to do a first-rate job of managing your company if you don't know what's going on and aren't familiar with the information being provided. *Appendix A contains a series of blank forms you may find helpful—one helps establish strategic and financial performance objectives, another can be used to do industry and competitive analysis, and one helps arrive at a company strategy.* Good luck, and we hope you enjoy playing *The Business Strategy Game.*

Planning and Analysis Forms

Provided in this section are several blank forms intended to help you organize and plan your company's strategy and operations, and analyze the industry in which you are competing.

Company Mission and Objectives

Mission Statement / Strategic Vision

Market Share Objectives

Private-Label Market ____ %

		Internet	Wholesale	
Branded ——	North America	____ %	____ %	____ %
Markets	Asia	____ %	____ %	____ %
	Europe	____ %	____ %	____ %
	Latin America	____ %	____ %	____ %

Overall Market Share ____ %

Long-Term Financial Performance Objectives

Growth in Revenues	____ %
Growth in Net Income	____ %
Growth in Earnings Per Share	____ %
Return on Investment	____ %
Bond Rating	____

Annual Financial Performance Objectives

	Year ___	Year ___	Year ___	Year ___	Year ___
Revenues	$ ____	$ ____	$ ____	$ ____	$ ____
Net Income	$ ____	$ ____	$ ____	$ ____	$ ____
Earnings Per Share	$ ____	$ ____	$ ____	$ ____	$ ____
Return On Investment	____ %	____ %	____ %	____ %	____ %
Bond Rating	____	____	____	____	____

Company Strategy

Primary Market Targets

Private-Label Market ☐

Branded Markets —— North America ☐

Asia ☐

Europe ☐

Latin America ☐

Rank from 1 to 5 in order of importance.

Overall Competitive Positioning

Check the appropriate boxes and fill in the blanks.

Price Relative to Competitors

Premium ☐

Above Average ☐

Average ☐

Below Average ☐

Lowest ☐

Service to Retailers

Superior ☐

Above Average ☐

Standard ☐

Rank in Industry ___

Product Line Breadth (models)

Broad ☐

Medium ☐

Narrow ☐

Rank in Industry ___

Number of Retail Outlets

Above Average ☐

Average ☐

Below Average ☐

Rank in Industry ___

Use of Customer Rebates

Heavy ☐

Medium ☐

Light ☐

Rank in Industry ___

Product Quality

Top of the Line ☐

Premium ☐

Good ☐

Acceptable ☐

Rank in Industry ___

Brand Image (image rating)

High Profile ☐

Moderate ☐

Low Profile ☐

Rank In Industry ___

Company-Owned Megastores

Above Average ☐

Average ☐

Below Average ☐

Rank In Industry ___

Advertising Budget

Above Average ☐

Average ☐

Below Average ☐

Rank In Industry ___

Online Sales Effort (internet market)

Strong ☐

Moderate ☐

Token ☐

None ☐

Overall Business Strategy

Check the appropriate box and explain.

Low-Cost ☐   **Competitive Advantage Being Sought** _____

Differentiation ☐ _____

Focus ☐ _____

Best-Cost ☐ _____

Actions to Gain Competitive Advantage

_____
_____
_____
_____
_____
_____
_____
_____
_____

Special Functional Area Strategies

Production
_____
_____
_____
_____
_____
_____
_____
_____

Marketing
_____
_____
_____
_____
_____
_____
_____
_____

Finance
_____
_____
_____
_____
_____
_____
_____

Human Resources
_____
_____
_____
_____
_____
_____
_____

Industry _____   *The Business Strategy Game*   Company _____

Industry and Competitive Analysis

Dominant Economic Characteristics

_____
_____
_____
_____
_____
_____
_____

Driving Forces

_____
_____
_____
_____
_____
_____
_____
_____

Assessment of Competitive Forces

_____
_____
_____
_____
_____
_____
_____
_____

Strength of Key Competitors

Rating Scale: 1 = weakest; 10 = strongest

Competitive Factor	Our Company	Key Competitors (company name or letter)						
Low-Cost	____	____	____	____	____	____	____	____
Quality	____	____	____	____	____	____	____	____
Service	____	____	____	____	____	____	____	____
Brand Image	____	____	____	____	____	____	____	____
Model Availability	____	____	____	____	____	____	____	____
Company Megastores	____	____	____	____	____	____	____	____
Retail Outlets	____	____	____	____	____	____	____	____
Management Expertise	____	____	____	____	____	____	____	____
Overall Strength Rating	____	____	____	____	____	____	____	____

Key Success Factors

_____

Industry Prospects / Overall Attractiveness

_____

Use the "Chart and Graph" option in the Analysis section of the Menu Bar to create strategic group maps for the North American, Asian, European, and Latin American markets. Create and attach any other graphs/charts necessary to complete your Industry and Competitive Analysis.